When the Thrill is Gone

How to Put the Life & Excitement Back Into ANY Relationship

by Stan Dubin

Based on the works of L. RON HUBBARD

Library of Congress Catalog Number: 99-93706

Copyright © 1999 Workable Solutions. All Rights Reserved. Quoted material by L. Ron Hubbard: © 1950, 1951, 1956, 1960, 1965, 1966, 1969, 1971, 1972, 1973, 1974, 1975, 1979, 1982, 1983, 1986, 1988, 1989, 1994, 1996 L. Ron Hubbard Library. Grateful acknowledgment is made to L. Ron Hubbard Library for permission to reproduce selections from the copyrighted works of L. Ron Hubbard. HUBBARD is a trademark and service mark owned by Religious Technology Center and used with its permission. The Way to Happiness is a trademark and service mark owned by L. Ron Hubbard Library. WISE I/A #9912270

ISBN 0-9662555-1-8

Important Note

In reading this book, be very certain you never go past a word you do not fully understand.

The only reason a person gives up a study or becomes confused or unable to learn is because he or she has gone past a word that was not understood.

The confusion or inability to grasp or learn comes AFTER a word that the person did not have defined and understood.

It may not only be the new and unusual words that you will have to look up. Some commonly used words can often be misdefined and so cause confusion.

This datum about not going past an undefined word is the most important factor in the whole subject of study. Every subject you have taken up and abandoned had its words which you failed to get defined.

Therefore, in reading this book be very, very certain you never go past a word you do not fully understand. If the material becomes confusing or you can't seem to grasp it, there will be a word just earlier that you have not understood. Don't go any further, but go back to BEFORE you got into trouble, find the misunderstood word and get it defined.

In keeping with the above Important Note, this book contains a glossary.

Words with an asterisk * next to them can be found in the glossary at the end of the book.

TABLE OF CONTENTS

CHAPTER 1...... Introduction 1

CHAPTER 2: ...... L. Ron Hubbard 5

CHAPTER 3: ...... Successful Applications 9

CHAPTER 4: ...... The Real Reason Relationships Fail 15

CHAPTER 5: ...... The Third Party 31

CHAPTER 6: ...... Cooling Things Off 37

CHAPTER 7: ...... Communication 41

CHAPTER 8: ...... Communication's Two Best Friends 49

CHAPTER 9: ...... Putting Order Into Your Relationships... 55

CHAPTER 10: ..... Freeing Yourself From The Past 59

CHAPTER 11: ..... Choosing Your People 67

CHAPTER 12: ..... The Emotional Tone Scale 71

CHAPTER 13: ..... The Chart Of Human Evaluation 81

CHAPTER 14: ..... Knowledge, Responsibility And Control .. 95

CHAPTER 15: ..... Increasing Your Ability To Confront ... 99

CHAPTER 16: ..... Help With The Kids 103

CHAPTER 17: ..... What Is Greatness? 109

CHAPTER 18: ..... Conclusion 111

                       Additional Services Available 113

                       Glossary 115

Dedication

This book could not have been remotely possible without L. Ron Hubbard.

I have been using Mr. Hubbard's materials for over 25 years. To this day, I am still awed at his unrelenting desire to improve the quality of life! The technology that he unselfishly developed over a lifetime of research has enriched the lives of millions. Every day, people from all walks of life, from all over the globe, benefit from Mr. Hubbard's materials. I thank him for the opportunity to provide a small portion of his works in this book!

I also want to thank my wife, Mary Ann. She has been an incredible source of support and unending love. Our marriage is in better shape now than it's ever been. And it gets better every day! She has always kept her eye on the mountain and together we are having a wonderful journey!

I am extremely thankful and proud to have Chelsea Dubin as my daughter. She wanted a strong and loving family to grow up into and she didn't just hope or wish for this. She, like her parents, worked on it. She contributed tremendous affinity*, reality and communication. And she continues to do so. The love of a child for one's parent has got to be one of the greatest feelings in all the world!

I'd like to also thank my good friend, Louis Swartz. Louis has a profound compassion for people and works tirelessly to help others live a better life. He has taught me many things and I am grateful for all of them.

Chapter One
INTRODUCTION

Do you remember how you felt when you started a very special relationship? Take a minute and think back to those first few days or weeks. Do you recall those strong emotions? Go back in your mind, back to the beginning of that relationship. Do you remember how eager you were to spend time with your new partner? Do you remember what it was like when you went to bed at night, thinking about this new person in your life? And then, when the morning came, this person was again in your thoughts?

Now perhaps that was not exactly how it happened for you. But you probably experienced something similar to it. You most likely did feel more alive. And I don't think it is a stretch to say you felt a real urge to care for this other person. And away you both went creating a new relationship and a new future.

Then time entered in. As the weeks became months and the months became years, these strong, vibrant feelings became less intense, less alive. In some cases, we still felt the desire to care for the other person, but the thrill was going away. That "loving feeling" had either weakened considerably or had gone away entirely.

Unfortunately for some of us, this meant that it was time to move on. The love had left the relationship, so we figured the relationship no longer should be continued. More unfortunate are those whose love, trust and caring turned eventually to hatred and suspicion.

How could such a wonderful beginning have such a bad ending?

What are the real forces at work that undermine our most treasured relationships? Are they identifiable? Can we know what causes a relationship to turn in the wrong direction? And more importantly, can we do something about it?

The answer is a very resounding YES!

The reasons a relationship goes off the rails have been discovered. And when I say 'discovered', I don't mean in some ivory tower* or psychobabble* sense. I mean the answers to any failing relationship have been discovered and put together in a way that YOU can use.

Many, many books have been written in an effort to improve relationships. Go into any bookstore and you'll see shelf after shelf of attempts to help you love and relate better. It's hard to miss the infomercials* promising to help couples improve their marriages.

So why is the divorce rate still wildly out of control? And why are there so many failed relationships?

Unfortunately, a great deal of the information on handling relationships is just plain false information.

Let's say a friend comes over and gives you a broken radio and asks you to fix it. The information you have on fixing radios is very limited, but you decide to give it a try. Perhaps you whack the side of the radio and it starts up, but a few minutes later it's on the blink again. If you knew the actual reasons why the radio was not working and you knew exactly what to do to fix the radio—well, you'd have a fixed radio in no time.

I realize it is a very bold statement to say that this book will deliver to you the reasons why your mate doesn't love you as much as he or she did a few months or years ago. But I don't mind being bold about a technology that works.

People do NOT just fall out of love. *Certain* things happened and when those exact things are located and addressed, a relationship can be dramatically improved. You will know why it went wrong and you will know how to make it go right.

The material in this book is based on the works of L. Ron Hubbard. Why? Very simply, because his technology works. Thousands upon thousands of people have successfully used his technology.

Mr. Hubbard once said,

> *"It's not man's dreams that fail him. It is the lack of know-how required to bring those dreams into actuality."*

This book will help you bring your dreams into actuality.

[Note: Any relationship will benefit from this book. Father and son. Mother and daughter. Brother and sister. Using the information in this book, even relationships between platonic friends can be strengthened or repaired. This book was written primarily for couples, but you will see that this information can be applied to any situation between two people.]

If you are beginning a new relationship, you will find sound and practical guidance through previously uncharted waters. You will appreciate knowing what the danger signs are and how to deal with them if/when they show up.

If you are out there looking for a new special someone, this book will give you crucial information that could make or break any future relationship!

If your relationship is just beginning to go in the wrong direction, read on! You will find new and powerful tools that will get things going in the right direction.

Even if you have given up all hope in salvaging your marriage or your relationship, this book can make a major difference.

This book can help you get back that "loving feeling".

And yes, you CAN get the thrill back!

Chapter Two

L. RON HUBBARD

March 13th is the day when L. Ron Hubbard was born. Today, 150 U.S. mayors and governors proclaim March 13th: "L. Ron Hubbard Day". This recognition is due to Mr. Hubbard's immense contributions to improving the quality of human life. He always felt a person could better his situation and better his prospects for the future.

Here are some of the areas that Mr. Hubbard made contributions to:

The Field of Education

After researching every sector of education, Mr. Hubbard found a major ingredient missing: the technology of study itself.

We all remember going through many years of education ... do you remember being taught HOW to study? Yes, we were told to read the first three chapters of our history book and that there will be a quiz. Were we given the exact details of how to study?

Are there specific principles associated with studying information? What are the barriers to study? How does one overcome these barriers?

Mr. Hubbard developed an exact technology of HOW to study. This study technology has been used by millions of students around the world. He discovered the primary barriers to study and he provided exact solutions to those barriers. And he discovered that study and education indeed had specific principles, which, if learned, would enable someone to study virtually anything and become proficient in that area.

In Mr. Hubbard's words:

> *"The end and goal of any society as it addresses the problem of education is to raise the ability, the initiative and the cultural level, and with all these,*

the survival level, of that society. And when a society forgets any one of these things it is destroying itself by its own educational mediums*."

Schools all over the world are utilizing Mr. Hubbard's study techniques. When the student learns HOW to study and starts succeeding in the wonderful process of learning, the symptoms that cause teachers and school "psychologists" to misdiagnose disappear. What is left is a student gaining knowledge*, learning skills, applying his information, increasing his and her survival.

More and more schools today are implementing the study and educational technology of Mr. Hubbard. It is a not a coincidence that these schools experience *very few* of the problems encountered in so many U.S. schools, including drug use and violence.

If you would like more information please refer to the back of the book. A booklet entitled "The Technology of Study" is available at nominal cost.

The Field of Drug Rehabilitation

Mr. Hubbard's drug rehabilitation methods are currently employed in seventy nations and are credited with the salvaging of a hundred thousand addicts.

Hubbard methods in this field have also helped over a million people to live drug-free lives and has helped countless people who were suffering the adverse effects of medicinal use.

His technology is considered the premier technology of drug rehabilitation.

If you are interested in more information on Mr. Hubbard's discoveries in the drug rehabilitation field, the booklet "Answers to Drugs" is now available. This booklet gives procedures to help get someone off of drugs and of course gives the straight scoop on the effects drugs have on the mind and the body. To obtain a copy of this booklet, please refer to the back of this book.

The Field of Criminal Reform

Mr. Hubbard made unique and powerful discoveries regarding the cause and prevention of crime. He wrote:

"If you want to rehabilitate a criminal, just go back and find out when he did lose his personal pride. Rehabilitate that one point and you don't have a criminal anymore."

The program that came out of Mr. Hubbard's research in this area is called "Criminon" and is used in over 300 prisons and penal institutions in 39 different states. This program uses no drugs or punitive* restraints, but rather addresses what Mr. Hubbard calls the basic goodness within all men.

Over 3,200 inmates have successfully participated in the Criminon program and are now living crime-free lives.

Author of a Common Sense Moral Code

Mr. Hubbard was keenly aware of the state of morals in today's society. But instead of complaining about it to others, Mr. Hubbard took it upon himself to write a common sense moral code. This moral code is known to many as "The Way to Happiness". Mr. Hubbard wrote this moral code in the form of a booklet that now has over 50 million copies in circulation in 18 different languages!

Containing 21 simple life-enhancing precepts, this moral code is completely non-religious in nature and is based solely on common sense. When people read the different precepts, it just makes good sense that applying this information will enhance their life. Moral codes that are forced on us are virtually useless. The Way to Happiness is a moral code that people enjoy putting into action.

In the United States, The Way to Happiness booklet forms the basis of the hugely successful "Set a Good Example Campaign" which has been used in over 7,000 schools and has involved over 5 million American students. For more information on the "Set a Good Example Campaign", call 310-764-2090 or visit their web site at http://www.cbaa.org.

For a copy of The Way to Happiness booklet, please refer to the back of this book.

The Arts

Mr. Hubbard was also extremely prolific* in the arts.

Mr. Hubbard's literary achievements are legendary. 35 of his books have appeared on international bestseller lists. The combined fiction and nonfiction sales of L. Ron Hubbard's books has reached to over 120 million copies.

His photography has received awards in various corners of the world.

He made breakthroughs in music that allowed renowned musicians even greater creativity.

He designed full length feature films and helped with the recording of musical albums.

Mr. Hubbard stated:

> *"A culture is only as great as its dreams, and its dreams are dreamed by artists."*

The Field of Administration

Mr. Hubbard did extensive research into how organizations work and how people can perform at their best within an organization. He has written literally thousands of pages on how to successfully run an organization of any size.

In the year 1996, over 76,000 businesses used Mr. Hubbard's technology.

The author has written a book entitled "The Small Business Success Manual" which draws from a number of Mr. Hubbard's principles on how to successfully run a business. To obtain a copy, please refer to the end of this book.

Improving The Quality Of Life

Mr. Hubbard is probably best known for his discoveries into Life itself. He has written over 40 books documenting these discoveries. He also gave several thousand lectures, most of which were recorded. His recorded lectures and books provide answers to many, many questions we all have: Who are we? What are our real capabilities? How can we succeed fully? Why do things not turn out the way we intend them to?

Many people would have you think that Life is very complex. A whole field of "experts" will tell you that the human mind is far too sophisticated for the "ordinary" person to understand. Mr. Hubbard discovered that Life is *not* complex and that the human mind can be understood by all of us.

Through the following chapters, you will learn many new pieces of information. This information was selected from the works of Mr. Hubbard. But the bottom line is and always will be: does it work?

Let's hear from a few people who have applied this information to their relationships ...

Chapter Three
SUCCESSFUL APPLICATIONS

"My wife and I have had some 'unexplainable' quarrels from time to time, and we couldn't sort out how to avoid it. We decided to apply some information from Mr. Hubbard's works. We learned how to handle what you do when you upset somebody. It was absolutely great, since what we used to do was the opposite ... we used to do such things as 'what happened, please explain, what was the upset ...' which made the upset last and grow. Mr. Hubbard's information was very, very helpful." — P.W.

♥ ♥ ♥

"I spent a lot of time in miserable relationships with the 'wrong' guy thinking that it was hopeless to be happy in a relationship, that I just couldn't choose the right person to be with. In reading over some material by L. Ron Hubbard, I found out not only why I was choosing these 'wrong' guys but how to choose the right guy. I discovered a lot about myself and cleaned up a lot of bad past relationships. As a bonus my relationship with my family improved and I finally figured out how to choose the right person, whether to be a husband or friend. I know it sounds mushy romantic but the funny thing is there was someone out there doing the same thing and when we 'found' each other we knew, 'this is it!' We have been very happily married for a year now!" —S.L.

♥ ♥ ♥

"I have been with my husband since 1966 and married since 1968. From my point of view, the keys to a successful relationship lie in understanding and using the material from L. Ron Hubbard. A relationship takes work to continually create. I won't say that our marriage has been perfect 100% of the time, but we've never gotten ourselves into anything we couldn't remedy by ourselves. I attribute that to our use of Mr. Hubbard's materials." — H.B.

"My husband and I have been married since 1985 and from the start we had some trouble actually 'meshing' together as a married couple. We had all sorts of conflicts, from small disagreements to full scale arguments and couldn't quite put our finger on what the trouble was. Then we decided to use some technology from L. Ron Hubbard that deals specifically with upsets in marriage. What we found out was that neither one of us had started to be married! So, neither one of us had ever really committed to making the marriage work! We had some things to work out between us, but since then everything has been getting better day by day. We can talk with each other without becoming upset or angry and really, really communicate with each other!" —S.S.

♥ ♥ ♥

"When my wife and I were considering marriage, we applied a piece of technology from L. Ron Hubbard. It worked beautifully. To date, marrying my wife is the best decision I've ever made. We made the decision to get married three weeks after I had met her. That was three years ago! Mr. Hubbard's technology made a huge difference in our lives!" — G.F.

♥ ♥ ♥

"I love being married. My husband is my best friend. We both routinely use L. Ron Hubbard's technology on relationships to resolve any hitches in our marriage. In fact, because we know the technology so well, we seldom have any hitches as we realize even before the problem starts that we don't need to create the problem, so it never really takes hold. With a good knowledge and application of L. Ron Hubbard's technology, a couple can be in control of their own happiness within a marriage." —T.A.

♥ ♥ ♥

"After learning about L. Ron Hubbard's Emotional Tone Scale in full and how it relates to other parts of one's life, I feel more able to recognize a responsible, able person than before. Before it was pot luck. This has been very helpful in relationships."

— R.J.

♥ ♥ ♥

"My wife and I went through a bad patch in our marriage a few years ago, basically heading for divorce as there were too many differences, it seemed. So we did the Marriage Counseling that is based on L. Ron Hubbard's data. This totally cleaned up the communication between us, enabling us to look at the situation cleanly. We are still together, four years later, happier then we ever have been and considering adding another person to our family! — I.H.

Chapter 3 — Successful Applications

"After my first marriage ended I applied a very powerful piece of technology from L. Ron Hubbard. I set up qualifications that a partner would have to meet and wrote down my ideal scene. Over the next two years I refined this whenever I would get into a relationship and it would end. The relationships I got into got shorter and shorter because it was clear early on that the two of us did not really align. Each of these relationships would end with us friends. Finally, I put one last finishing touch to these qualifications and the ideal scene and within a week I met the lady who I am now very happily married to. We are so aligned it's incredible. We've been together 5 years now and every day it just gets better and better — hey, that was in my ideal scene — well, wha-da-ya-know!"

—G.S.

♥ ♥ ♥

"Before Lisa and I got married, we sat down and applied a key principle developed by L. Ron Hubbard. We worked out each of the different 'hats' that are worn in a relationship, and from that point forward, we were able to avoid that problem area completely. Cut to 5 years later and, although we have had some noisy spots from time to time, there has never been an instance of finger-pointing or upset over who should have done what around the house, etc."

— B.D.

♥ ♥ ♥

"When my husband and I decided to date and were considering marriage, we utilized information from L. Ron Hubbard's works to determine whether we would be a good couple. The information we used helped us to determine that we both have very similar goals and purposes for the future and that we met what each other wanted in a spouse. As our relationship grew and we became married, we continued to use Mr. Hubbard's works to strengthen our communication between ourselves and with our children. By doing this it increased our closeness and created a very open environment for our children to feel free to talk to us about what they wanted or needed to talk about. I firmly believe that the root of our happy family and it's successful future lie in the materials that we continually use from Mr. Hubbard's work. We apply his principles from the basics of improving communication through organizing how we manage our home with all the activities that we and our six children are involved in. I don't believe we could have a sane, happy household without all the assistance we have through the use of this information."

— B.S.

"My husband and I had grown apart and as a result we had quite a few confrontations and there was a lot of very tense feeling about our marriage. So we decided to have the marriage counseling that L. Ron Hubbard developed. It was really excellent. Such a very simple process with so much power applied right to the root of the problem which enabled us to confront the situation. It was so pleasant, we could both see that this was the way to handle it. I would recommend to do these actions to anyone that has been married for any length of time or no length of time (either)... it is a must for any relationship to endure and flourish."
— A.D.

♥ ♥ ♥

"My husband and I are celebrating our 20th wedding anniversary this very day! The cold, hard fact is that we never would have made it without the relationship tools we have both learned from the technology of L. Ron Hubbard. Each year our relationship gets better and stronger, with more understanding. We have a tremendously stable marriage knowing that we can trust each other fully in all things which has provided a wonderful foundation for both of us to enjoy and create the other areas of our lives."
—B.S.

♥ ♥ ♥

"I had been married and divorced and considered that I did not have good enough judgment to choose a good husband. I was too naive, nice, etc. and was taken advantage of in the past. I also had many disasters and failures as a mother both with my daughter and three children I lost before birth. Then I received some counseling. This was counseling based on material of L. Ron Hubbard. I found out that there were things that I was either completely unaware of or only slightly aware of. This counseling helped me to understand all of my previous disasters and failures with marriage and relationships. Immediately upon returning home from getting this counseling, I got back into communication with my ex-boyfriend. What the counseling did was eliminate the cause of why I couldn't have a good relationship and brought me up to a level where I could create a lasting and desirable relationship. Being able to have pleasure in this area with a total absence of upset and turmoil was a whole new experience for me and one which I am still taking full advantage of every day. We married a little over a year later and are doing great!"
— J.S.

"*My husband and I did the marriage counseling that was developed by L. Ron Hubbard. The biggest thing that occurred was that we found (and have kept) a huge affinity for each other. I personally remember thinking how the simplest things - uncommunicated - could cause such distress. Much of what he revealed was already known by me, but the fact of their not having been revealed was what made them painful for him. And watching someone with that much upset come through it was wonderful.*"

— L.T.

♥ ♥ ♥

"*My wife and I had been going to 'group counseling' for several years. During that time we would sometimes drive away from the group meetings feeling a little better about each other, but there were also times when we would come home mad at each other, not even talking on the drive home from the group. But we were persistent and kept on hoping that things would work out.*

"*When introduced to Mr. Hubbard's marriage counseling program, it made sense and we more or less said, 'What have we got to lose?' If we didn't do something we were either going to split or lead lives of quiet desperation 'for the children's sake.' After this marriage counseling, we were assured that Mr. Hubbard had solved the problem with marriages. Our marriage was now better than it had ever been, and it didn't take years; it only took hours. As we could see that the other things we had been doing were nearly useless, we resigned from the marriage group and in our resignation letter recommended that all the couples remaining get some of the same marriage counseling my wife and I had received.*

"*As a result of this marriage counseling, we learned what had been causing the trouble for all those years. It's now been 8 years since our marriage counseling and there is no doubt about whether we will make it as a couple. I urge anyone who has any trouble with their marriage, whether great or not so great, to get the marriage counseling based on Mr. Hubbard's technology. It will help you tremendously.*"

— G.C.

♥ ♥ ♥

"*My husband and I had lost interest in each other about a year and a half after our marriage. We couldn't figure out what had happened. We had just drifted apart. Now, using Mr. Hubbard's techniques, we have found romance again — something, I thought we'd completely lost sight of.*"

— K.D.

Chapter Four

THE REAL REASON RELATIONSHIPS FAIL

"How did we fall out of love?" "How did things go so far off the rails?" "How could we have been so much in love and now ...."

A new relationship is filled with so many wonderful qualities: hope, promise, passion, pleasure, security. What should we do when the passion starts to fade? What do we do when the hope and promise is no longer present? And when the very security of the relationship is threatened, what steps can we take to turn things around?

Well, first things first. We need to know the real reason relationships begin to go wrong and eventually go very wrong. And we need to have a very good grasp of this information. When you know THE MAJOR reason why a relationship goes off the rails, you will have in your possession a powerful tool to fix things.

Before we go any further, let me tell you what *isn't* the key reason:

- It's NOT because you're having money problems.
- It's NOT because the husband is working long hours.
- It's NOT because the wife has a career.
- It's NOT because "you're going in different directions".
- It's NOT because your spouse no longer really pays attention to you.
- It's NOT because one or both of you "need some space."
- It's NOT due to less (or no) lovemaking.

All of the above may be factors, but they are not THE KEY REASON.

This chapter will give you THE major reason a relationship starts well and then goes sour. You may think at first that this explanation is too simple. But read all the way through this chapter. With this chapter, you have your hands on THE MAJOR REASON relationships fail, or even begin to fail.

So, let's get down to it.

Over the years, each one of us has done things that we know we shouldn't have done. Some "small" things, some things not so small. Maybe the husband said he was at work late one night, when he was really out with the guys ... and he didn't tell his wife that he was out with the guys.

No big deal, you say? Maybe. Maybe not.

Perhaps the wife spent some money on an item that wasn't really needed, knowing the family needed other more important things. And then she didn't tell her husband that she did this.

Not the end of the world, right? Certainly not the end of the world, but when these kind of things accumulate, they can eventually have a very adverse effect on the relationship.

For now, we will call these things "transgressions." We will define a transgression simply as something we should not have done.

The Agreements We Make

When people decide to get together, either in a relationship or in any kind of group situation, they make certain agreements with each other.

In a work situation, we usually agree to be on time, to work hard, to be as productive as possible.

In a relationship, we usually agree to be sexually faithful, to be honest, to be supportive.

We may not sit down and list out all of these agreements, but these agreements are there. They may not have been put in writing, they may not even have been *formally* agreed upon, but they do exist.

When we do something that violates any of these agreements, we KNOW that we've done so. We may try to convince ourselves that "it was unavoidable" or that "he/she deserved it"—it doesn't matter. We know that we've done something that, in some way, has violated an agreement of the relationship.

Some of these transgressions are more serious than others. The husband might've been out with another woman that night he said he was working late. Or the wife could've taken a good amount of money and salted it away in an account the husband knows nothing about.

Usually, the more serious the transgression, the more unwilling we are to communicate it to our spouse. We tend to accumulate these transgressions over a period of time AND too often we keep them to ourselves.

Committing these transgressions is one thing. Then withholding (not communicating) what we did—this combination can have a very negative effect on a relationship.

When this kind of thing occurs over a period of years, the result is a lessened willingness to communicate and a reduced eagerness to be with each other. And from this condition, all kinds of other problems show up. But what came first was the withheld transgression(s).

[Note: While reading this chapter, you might start to feel uncomfortable. If this occurs, it means that certain things in your past are getting stirred up. Don't worry! Keep reading! Towards the end of the chapter you will be given a procedure that will give tremendous relief.]

Those Things We Should've Done

Now, there is another type of transgression. These are things that we should've done, but we didn't. These "omissions★" have a similar adverse effect.

Example: let's say the kids are fighting and the mom knows that she should go in and break it up. But she decides not to and one of the kids breaks a lamp. Had the mom gone in and settled things down, we'd still have a good lamp. She "omitted" to take the action of breaking up the fight.

Example: the father notices that the older daughter has some signs of taking drugs. The father knows what these telltale signs are and the daughter *is* exhibiting some of these signs. But he ignores them. He doesn't sit down with his daughter and have a heart-to-heart with her. He decides "maybe I didn't really see what I thought I saw." Or he figures "nah, not my daughter." A few weeks later, the daughter gets arrested with some of her friends. Drugs are involved.

The father "omitted" to sit down with his daughter and get into sufficient communication with her to determine that 1) she is not involved with drugs in any way or 2) if she is, he works with her to get this resolved!

I am not trying to give you examples of what may be happening to you. I just want you to understand how this type of transgression can occur. The person knows he or she should take some action and then doesn't.

Perhaps the husband knew his wife needed some help one night. She was coughing and coughing, but the husband pretended to be asleep not wanting to get up and help her. This "omitted action" is in fact a type of transgression.

These transgressions involve things that we should have done but didn't —and they have a similar negative effect that the other type of transgression has.

Here is an interesting quote from the works of L. Ron Hubbard:

> *"People, then, in forming groups, create a series of agreements of what is right and what is wrong, what is moral and what is immoral, what is survival and what is nonsurvival. That is what is created. And then this disintegrates* by transgressions (violations of agreements or laws). These transgressions, unspoken but nevertheless transgressions, by each group member gradually mount up to a disintegration."*
>
> *"These transgressions and their effects have been examined in great detail…*
>
> *"A harmful act or a transgression against the moral code of a group is called an* overt act. *When a person does something that is contrary to the moral code he has agreed to, or when he omits to do something that he should have done per that moral code, he has committed an overt act. An overt act violates what was agreed upon.*
>
> *"An unspoken, unannounced transgression against a moral code by which the person is bound is called a* withhold. *A withhold is an overt act a person committed that he or she is not talking about. It is something a person believes that, if revealed, will endanger his self-preservation. Any withhold comes* after *an overt act. Thus, an overt act is something* done*; a withhold is an overt act* withheld *from another or others.*

Let's go over these two new terms again:

An overt act is something that was done that in some way violates an agreement between two or more people. It could also be an "omission" to do something that should have been done.

A withhold is an overt act that the person is not talking about. The withhold comes after the overt act.

Here are two examples:

Overt: A man puts a quarter in a newspaper vending machine and takes *two* newspapers out of the machine and gives one to his friend.

Withhold: A man comes up to the cashier to purchase a sweater and the cash register rings up an amount that is less than what the sweater actually costs. The man knows this but does not mention this to the cashier.

Making the Other Person Look Bad

Often what happens after a person has committed overts, he or she feels the need to make the other person look bad.

"I don't come home on time anymore because my wife gained 30 pounds and just isn't the same woman I married!"

"I had the affair because my stupid husband wasn't paying attention to me!"

"I spent all that money on the cellular phone because my insensitive husband doesn't talk to me anymore!"

"My wife used to make me great dinners. Now she can't cook her way out of a paper bag!"

"I was a fool when I married you!"

There are all kinds of ways that a person justifies their own overts and withholds, but that is all it is — justification.

Quoting again from Mr. Hubbard's works:

> *"When a person has committed an overt act and then withholds it, he or she usually employs the social mechanism*of justification. By 'justification' we mean explaining how an overt act was not really an overt act.*
>
> *"We have all heard people attempt to justify their actions and all of us have known instinctively that justification amounted to a confession of guilt. But not until now have we understood the exact mechanism behind justification.*
>
> *"Previous to this technology, there was no means by which a person could relieve himself of consciousness of having done an overt act, except to try to lessen the overt.*

"Some churches and other groups have used confession in an effort to relieve a person of the pressure of his overt acts. However, lacking a full understanding of all the mechanisms at play, it has had limited workability. ...

"Withholds are a sort of overt act in themselves but have a different source. We have proven conclusively that man is basically good—a fact which flies in the teeth of older beliefs that man is basically evil. Man is good to such an extent that when he realizes he is being very dangerous and in error he seeks to minimize his power and if that doesn't work and he still finds himself committing overt acts he then seeks to dispose of himself either by leaving or by getting caught.

"People withhold overt acts because they conceive that telling them would be another overt act.

"In view of these mechanisms, when the burden became too great, man was driven to another mechanism—the effort to lessen the size and pressure of the overt. He or she could only do this by attempting to reduce the size and repute of the person against whom the overt was committed. Hence, when a man or a woman has done an overt act, there usually follows an effort to reduce the goodness or importance of the target of the overt. Hence, the husband who betrays his wife must then state that the wife was no good in some way. Thus, the wife who betrayed her husband had to reduce the husband to reduce the overt. In this light, most criticism is justification of having done an overt.

"This is a downward spiral. One commits overt acts unwittingly. He then seeks to justify them by finding fault or displacing blame. This leads him into further overts against the same people which leads to degradation of himself and sometimes those people.

"When you hear scathing* and brutal criticism of someone which sounds just a bit strained*, know that you have your eye on overts against that criticized person.

"We now have technology that includes the factual explanation of departures, sudden and relatively unexplained, from jobs, families, locations and areas. These departures are called blow-offs.

"This is one of the things man thought he knew all about and therefore never bothered to investigate. Yet this amongst all other things gave him the most trouble. Man had it all explained to his own satisfaction and yet his

explanation did not cut down the amount of trouble which came from the feeling of 'having to leave.'

"For instance, man has been frantic about the high divorce rate, about the high job turnover in plants, about labor unrest and many other items, all stemming from the same source—sudden departures or gradual departures.

"We have the view of a person who has a good job, who probably won't get a better one, suddenly deciding to leave and going. We have the view of a wife with a perfectly good husband and family leaving it all. We see a husband with a pretty and attractive wife breaking up the affinity and departing.

"Man explained this to himself by saying that things were done to him which he would not tolerate and therefore he had to leave. But if this were the explanation, all man would have to do would be to make working conditions, marital relationships, jobs, training programs and so on all very excellent and the problem would be solved. But on the contrary, a close examination of working conditions and marital relationships demonstrates that improvement of conditions often worsens the amount of blow-off.

"Probably the finest working conditions in the world were achieved by Mr. Hershey of chocolate bar fame for his plant workers. Yet they revolted and even shot at him. This in its turn led to an industrial philosophy that 'the worse workers were treated, the more willing they were to stay,' which in itself is as untrue as 'the better they are treated, the faster they blow off.'

"One can treat people so well that they grow ashamed of themselves, knowing they don't deserve it, that a blow-off is precipitated*. And, certainly, one can treat people so badly that they have no choice but to leave. But these are extreme conditions and in between these we have the majority of departures: The wife is doing her best to make a marriage and the husband wanders off on the trail of a promiscuous woman. The manager is trying to keep things going and the worker leaves. These, the unexplained, disrupt organizations and lives and it's time we understood them.

"People leave because off their own overts and withholds. That is the factual fact and the hard-bound rule. A man with a clean heart can't be hurt. The man or woman who must, must, must become a victim and depart is departing because of his or her own overts and withholds. It

> *doesn't matter whether the person is departing from a town or a job. The cause is the same.*
>
> *"Almost anyone, no matter his position and no matter what is wrong can remedy a situation if he or she really wants to. When the person no longer wants to remedy it, his own overt acts and withholds against the others involved in the situation have lowered his own ability to be responsible for it. Therefore, departure is the only apparent answer. To justify the departure, the person blowing off dreams up things done to him, in an effort to minimize the overt by degrading those it was done to. The mechanics* involved are quite simple.*
>
> *"All a divorce is, or all an inclination* or a withdrawal is, is simply too many overts and withholds against the marital partner. It's as uncomplicated as that.*
>
> *"When a marital partner is straining or wanting to leave and saying 'I ought to go' or 'I ought to do something else' or 'We ought to split up' or 'I'd be much better off if we hadn't', all of those rationales* stem immediately from the overt acts and withholds of the partner making those rationales against the other partner."*

Let me repeat one line from above:

> *"All a divorce is, or all an inclination or a withdrawal is, is simply too many overts and withholds against the marital partner."*

So if either you or your spouse are experiencing an inclination to split up or go separate ways, what do you know is *actually* happening? You know that such an inclination is the result of too many overts and withholds against the other partner.

What if you or your partner are starting to withdraw? What do you know? You know that the person withdrawing has too many overts and withholds against the other partner.

I realize this information may be new to you. I also realize that you may feel that the problem is "over there". In other words, you may be thinking similar thoughts to these:

- "He doesn't care for me anymore. Why should I stay with him?"

- "She doesn't make love to me anymore! I should consider going elsewhere!"

- "He doesn't show any affection. He used to. It's hard to be with someone who doesn't show affection!"

What is the common denominator* of all of these thoughts?

The Problem is Over There!

Yes, it takes two to tangle. But the source of your upset with your partner is NOT what your partner has done to you.

Let me make a suggestion here. Go back to the beginning of this chapter and read it again up to this point. Get yourself even more familiar with the concepts being explained here. Get a very good idea of what an overt is, what a withhold is. I really want you to understand why a person starts to withdraw or wants to leave a relationship.

Do you have any friends who are very critical of their spouses? Do they go on and on about how horrible the husband is, or every other word you hear out of them is a negative criticism of the wife? Know this: the person making these remarks has very simply accumulated his or her own overts and withholds and those overts and withholds are the sole source of these continual complaints.

I am not saying there are no valid complaints. Of course there are.

But when a person has not accumulated overts and withholds, they have a different viewpoint of the faults of their spouse. They have a lighter viewpoint, a more constructive viewpoint, a more caring viewpoint. The willingness to remedy the scene still exists. As the overts and withholds accumulate, this lighthearted, constructive, caring viewpoint fades and the scene may even eventually get ugly.

But it doesn't matter how ugly it gets. It can be turned around.

Writing up Your Overts and Withholds

So, let's get started on repairing things for you. I want you to get out some paper and I want you to write up your own overts and withholds. This will accomplish several things:

- It will clear the air for you personally. You will have a better understanding of why you feel the way you do.

- It will give you a new perspective on the other half of the relationship. You will have a better understanding of where he or she is coming from.

- You will experience significant relief … relief from some of the stress of the relationship.

The terms overt and withhold can also be abbreviated to O/W.

There is a very specific procedure for writing up one's overts and withholds. From Mr. Hubbard's works:

"Overts are the biggest reason a person restrains* and withholds himself from action.

"A person who has overts and withholds becomes less able to influence his own life and the lives of others around him and falls out of communication with those people and things he has committed overts against.

"Writing up one's overts and withholds offers a road out. By confronting the truth an individual can experience relief and a return of responsibility*.

"The format for doing an O/W write-up is as follows:

"1. Write down the exact overt of commission or omission.

"2. Then state explicitly the specifics regarding the action or inaction, including:

"a. Time (Definition: a precise instant, second, minute, hour, day, week, month or year, determined by clock or calendar; the point at which something has happened.)

"b. Place (Definition: a definite location.)

"c. Form (Definition: the arrangement of things; the way in which parts of a whole are organized.)

"d. Event (Definition: that which happens; result; any incident or occurrence.)

"One has to get the time, place, form and event, and one has to get a done (action done) or a failure (to do some action) in order to get a full resolution.

"Example:

" '1. I hit a friend's car when backing out of my parking space at work and caused about five hundred dollars worth of damage to his car.

" '2. On the 30th of June 1987, when I was leaving work, I was backing out of my parking space and hit the back end of my friend Joe's car. There was no one else around and the parking lot was almost empty. I drove away without leaving a note or telling Joe, knowing that I caused about five hundred dollars damage to his car which he had to pay for.*

"*or, when there is a withhold or withholds to be gotten off:*

"*1. Write down the withhold.*

"*2. Then state explicitly the specifics regarding the action or inaction withheld, including:*

"*a. Time*

"*b. Place*

"*c. Form*

"*d. Event*

"*For example:*

" '1. I cheated on my wife (Sally) by seeing another woman and never told her about this.*

" '2. Three years ago, when I was first married to Sally, I cheated on her by seeing another woman. I have never told Sally about this. One morning (in June 1985) I had told Sally I would take her to the movies that night and on my way home from work, when I was at Jones' Department Store, I saw an old girlfriend of mine (Barbara). I asked Barbara to go out to dinner with me that night and she accepted. (She did not know that I was married.) I told her I would pick her up at 8:00 P.M. that night. When I got home from the store I told Sally I had to go back to work to get some things done and would not be able to go to the movies with her.*

" 'I then went out to dinner in another city with Barbara (at the Country Inn) so that I would not risk seeing any of my friends.'*

You will notice in the two examples above, the first thing you do is *state what the overt or withhold is*. Then you give the *full* data on the overt or withhold, which includes when it happened (time); where it happened (place); the arrangement of things or the way the parts of the whole are organized (form); and what actually happened, the result, the incident itself (event).

Time, Place, Form and Event Spells Relief!

You are keenly interested in writing down the time, place, form and event. This gives the complete story on what happened. In order to get the full benefits from this activity, you need to give the full details of what actually occurred.

Here are some more examples of overts and withholds that could be written up (these are not actual overts and withholds, but they will give more understanding of how to do this write-up):

1. I bought a cooked meal from one of the local caterers and gave my husband the impression that I cooked the entire meal.

2. This took place about 3 years ago, in the spring. My husband had asked me to cook a really sensational meal because he wanted to impress his boss. So the day came when I was supposed to cook this great meal. In the afternoon, from my house, I called the caterer and asked them to prepare a meal for 4 people and to bring it by the house no later than 4:30. They brought the dinner over in time, and I then placed a part of it in the oven and the rest of it I put into various dishes. Around 5PM, my husband came home with his boss and the boss's wife. After talking for about 10-15 minutes and after a drink or two, I asked everybody to come into the dining room. I then took the food that was in the oven and put that into a big dish. I actually made a slight moan while leaning over into the oven so that I would draw some attention to the fact that I was pulling the food out of the oven. During the meal, the boss's wife commented on how good a cook I am. My husband gave me an appreciative look. I never told him that I had not cooked the meal myself.

Another example:

1. I stayed up late one night and watched an X rated movie.

2. About four months ago, Shelly and I had agreed that I would no longer watch these kinds of movies. But about 2 weeks after we had made that agreement, I went out to a video store and rented one. I brought the movie home, but kept it hidden in the car. After Shelly fell asleep around 11 o'clock, I went to the car and got the movie. I popped it into the VCR in the den and turned the sound all the way down so Shelly wouldn't hear anything. I shut the door to the den and then sat down and watched the movie which had all kinds of sexually explicit scenes in it. I watched many scenes of lovemaking and I got turned on sexually while doing so. After the movie was over, I took it out of the VCR and put it back into my car, under the car seat. I returned the video the next morning on my way to work. I never told Shelly about this.

Another example:

1. I told my wife I was going to be late at the office, but instead I went to an ice hockey game.

2. Three weeks ago, I called home to my wife Becky and told her that work was piling up at the office and that I needed to stay late to catch up on it. I remember closing the door to my office so that none of my associates would hear this phone call. I then called Frank, my best friend, and told him I was ready to go to the game. Frank came by the office, picked me up and away we went to the ice hockey game. After the game, Frank dropped me off at my office and I drove home from there. I never told Becky about this.

Another example:

1. I broke a promise to my husband.

2. Last summer, I took the kids to an amusement park. My husband, Bill, gave me $40 for the whole day. Our finances were very tight and he made me promise that I wouldn't spend more than the $40. I promised I would keep it under $40. When we got to the amusement park, the $40 was gone in 30 minutes. I had two choices at that point: I could just let the kids walk around the park and do nothing that cost money or I could get this $20 bill out of my purse and spend that on them. I took the $20 and spent that. When I got home, Bill asked how it went and I very nervously replied, "Great" and then quickly went into the kitchen. I was very quiet the rest of the night. I withheld from Bill that I had spent more than we agreed.

Those examples give you an idea of what this write-up should consist of.

What Kinds of Things Should YOU Write Up?

Whatever comes to your mind that is an overt or a withhold.

It is not a bad idea to read over the first section of this chapter several times. The more certain you are of these concepts, the easier it will be to do this write-up.

Remember, you and your spouse have certain agreements with each other. It doesn't matter whether you actually sat down and worked out these agreements. YOU KNOW what these agreements are. Any violations of these agreements would qualify for this write-up.

Mr. Hubbard goes on to say:

"The action of writing up one's overts and withholds can be applied to anyone, and the breadth* of its application is unlimited....

"In doing an O/W write-up a person writes up his overts and withholds until he is satisfied that they are complete. The person will feel very good about it and experience relief. One would not engage in carrying on an O/W write-up past this point.

"Writing up one's overts and withholds is a simple procedure with unlimited application. A husband and wife could write up their overts and withholds on their marriage. An employee could write up his O/Ws concerning his job. A rebellious student could write down his transgressions at school.

"One can straighten out any area of life by coming to grips* once and for all with one's violations against the various moral codes to which he agreed and later transgressed. The relief which can accompany the unburdening of one's misdeeds is often very great. One can again feel a part of a group or relationship and regain respect for oneself, the trust and friendship of others and a great deal of personal happiness.

"This is extremely useful technology."

After you've written up your overts and withholds and have experienced some well-deserved relief, what should you do next? Well, do your darndest to get your spouse (or boyfriend/girlfriend, or son/daughter) to write up his or her overts and withholds! The purpose in doing this write-up is to improve the scene and to increase the quality of communication between the two of you. If your spouse is totally unwilling to do this write-up, don't let that prevent you from doing it. The benefits to YOU are worth the effort and you will be able to bring those benefits to the relationship in many different ways.

Remember, you are not required to give the write-up to your partner to read.

VERY IMPORTANT NOTE: If you and your partner do decide to show each other your write-ups, you must, must, must agree ahead of time to simply read them and then acknowledge* each other for what you've done. The whole purpose of this action is to help improve communication. If you read your spouse's O/W write-up, one or both of you may be inclined to get into "look what you've done to me!" or "I can't believe you did those things!" You must not get into recriminations. Your self-restraint here is very important.

If you do decide to show these write-ups to each other and if either or both of you find yourself blaming the other or finding fault with the other, realize one very important thing: you have more overts and withholds to write up! When these are fully written up, the attitude changes. To reiterate* what Mr. Hubbard said earlier:

> *"This is a downward spiral. One commits overt acts unwittingly. He then seeks to justify them by finding fault or displacing blame.*
>
> *"When you hear scathing and brutal criticism of someone which sounds just a bit strained, know that you have your eye on overts against that criticized person."*

The O/W Write-up is a very powerful tool. Use it exactly the way it is laid out and you will experience excellent benefits!

*C*hapter *F*ive

THE THIRD PARTY*

There is another very important factor that can cause a relationship to go sour. This is the factor of a "third party", a person outside of the relationship who, in some way, is causing a problem inside the relationship.

This is a person that is promoting conflict between the two partners and is doing so in a way that is not always easily detectable by either of the partners.

Here is some key data from L. Ron Hubbard on this subject:

> *"Violence and conflict amongst individuals and nations have been with us for ages and their causes have remained a complete mystery.*
>
> *"If Babylon could turn to dust, if Egypt could become a badlands*, if Sicily could have 160 prosperous cities and be a looted ruin before the year zero and a near desert ever since—and all this in* spite *of all the work and wisdom and good wishes and intent of human beings, then it must follow as the dark follows sunset that something must be unknown to man concerning all his works and ways. And that this something must be so deadly and so pervasive as to destroy all his ambitions and his chances long before their time.*
>
> *"Such a thing would have to be some natural law unguessed at by himself.*
>
> *"And there* is *such a law, apparently, that answers these conditions of being deadly, unknown and embracing all activities.*
>
> *"The law would seem to be:*
>
> *"A THIRD PARTY MUST BE PRESENT AND UNKNOWN IN EVERY QUARREL FOR A CONFLICT TO EXIST.*
>
> *"or*

"FOR A QUARREL TO OCCUR, AN UNKNOWN THIRD PARTY MUST BE ACTIVE IN PRODUCING IT BETWEEN TWO POTENTIAL OPPONENTS.

"or

"WHILE IT IS COMMONLY BELIEVED TO TAKE TWO TO MAKE A FIGHT, A THIRD PARTY MUST EXIST AND MUST DEVELOP IT FOR ACTUAL CONFLICT TO OCCUR.

"It is very easy to see that two in conflict are fighting. They are very visible. What is harder to see or suspect is that a third party existed and actively promoted the quarrel.

"The usually unsuspected and 'reasonable' third party, the bystander who denies any part of it, is the one that brought the conflict into existence in the first place.

"The hidden third party, seeming at times to be a supporter of only one side, is to be found as the instigator.

"This is a useful law in many areas of life…

"One sees two fellows shouting bad names at each other, sees them come to blows.

"No one else is around. So they, of course, 'caused the fight.' But there was a third party.

"Tracing these down, one comes upon incredible data. That is the trouble. The incredible is too easily rejected. One way to hide things is to make them incredible.

"Farmer J and Rancher K have been tearing each other to pieces for years in continual conflict. There are obvious, logical reasons for the fight. Yet it continues and does not resolve. A close search finds Banker L who, due to their losses in the fighting, is able to loan each side money while keeping the quarrel going, and who will get their lands completely if both lose.

"One looks over 'personal' quarrels, group conflicts, national battles and one finds, if he searches, the third party, unsuspected by both combatants or, if suspected at all, brushed off as 'fantastic.' Yet careful documentation finally affirms it.

"This datum is fabulously useful.

"In marital quarrels the correct approach of anyone counseling is to get both parties to carefully search out the third party. They may come to many reasons at first. These reasons are not people. One is looking for a third party, an actual person. When both find the third party and establish proof, that will be the end of the quarrel.

"Sometimes two parties, quarreling, suddenly decide to elect a person to blame. This stops the quarrel. Sometimes it is not the right person and more quarrels thereafter occur.

"Marital conflicts are common. Marriages can be saved by both parties really sorting out who caused the conflicts. There may have been, in the whole history of the marriage several, but only one at a time.

"There are no conflicts which cannot be resolved unless the true promoters of them remain hidden."

So, let's take a look at this. Mr. Hubbard says: *"In marital quarrels the correct approach of anyone counseling is to get both parties to carefully search out the third party. They may come to reasons at first. These reasons are not people. One is looking for a third party, an actual person."*

Finding the Third Party

How do you go about this? Fortunately, a very exact procedure was developed that will find this third party. Here is the procedure from Mr. Hubbard's works:

"How to Find a Third Party

"The way not to find a third party is to compile a questionnaire that asks, 'Have you been a victim?' Do not ask questions such as, 'Who has been mean to you?' or other questions which would tend to elicit* answers that the person has been victimized*. This kind of question will not locate the individual stirring up conflicts between people.

"By definition, a third party is one who by false reports creates trouble between two people, a person and a group or a group and another group.

"The object of the investigation, then, is to find out who has been spreading false reports in order to stir up conflicts between people or groups. To find a third party one has to ask those involved in the dispute questions along the following lines:

> *"1a. Have you been told you were in bad?*
>
> *"b. What was said?*
>
> *"c. Who said it?*
>
> *"2a. Have you been told someone was bad?*
>
> *"b. What was said?*
>
> *"c. Who said it?*
>
> *"3a. Have you been told someone was doing wrong?*
>
> *"b. What was said?*
>
> *"c. Who said it?*
>
> *"4a. Have you been told a group was bad?*
>
> *"b. What was said?*
>
> *"c. Who said it?*
>
> *"This questionnaire may have a lot of answers so leave ample space for each question. By then combining names given, you have one name appearing far more often than the rest. This is done by counting names.*
>
> *"By following this procedure, you will find out exactly who has been stirring up conflicts and thus open the door to their resolution.*
>
> *"With this tool in your hands you will be able to change conditions between family members, associates and groups you come into contact with and restore harmony.*

If this is being done with you and your spouse, the questions should all start out: "In your marriage ..." Only the first three sets of questions need to be used.

If it's being done for a boyfriend/girlfriend relationship, each question should start out: "In your relationship ..." Once again, use only the first three sets of questions.

If you're applying this to a family situation, each question should start with: "In this family ..."

The way this should be done is to get someone outside of the relationship to sit down with both you and your spouse. The person you choose needs to study the information in this chapter and then sit down and ask each of the questions above.

Remember, leave ample space as there may be many answers.

Then Mr. Hubbard says, *"By then combining names given, you have one name appearing far more often than the rest. This is done by counting names."*

After you locate the "third party" whose name came up far more often than the rest, what do you do about this person? Well, first of all, learning that this individual has been busy promoting conflict is usually a major revelation. This alone can provide tremendous relief.

Often this person is not suspected as a trouble source ... but doing this investigation will prove otherwise.

Sometimes one partner is aware of this other person as a source of trouble, but the other partner doesn't buy it. Once again, using this questionnaire will prove very insightful.

What to Do With What You Found

How you handle this "third party" will depend on several things. If this person does not have a close relationship with either partner, you may want to consider not associating with this person. But if this person has a close relationship with either of the partners (for example, a family member), then one approach is to sit down and let this person know that you've conducted an investigation into some of the troubles in your relationship and inform this person that he/she has been found to be promoting conflict and that you would like this person to stop doing this.

Or you may decide not to say anything at all to this person. And then if/when the person says something derogatory later up the line - you confront the person right then and there and say, "Hey, Judy, I don't want you making any more derogatory remarks about my husband! You've made a bunch of comments in the past and my mistake was to listen to them... I'm working on improving my relationship with my husband and it would be very helpful if you understood that and stopped making negative comments about him."

You may even take that conversation one step further and say, "And, Judy, when you're talking to my husband, please refrain from making derogatory comments about me!"

Whatever conversation you decide to have with the "third party" be prepared for some very interesting results. The person may feel very indignant and hurt. But if this person is the correct third party, they will know that they have been found out. And things should settle down considerably.

Also, keep in mind a gesture can be a powerful communication. For instance, if you're talking to a friend of yours and you mention something about your husband and your friend frowns, the intention behind this frown may be: 'well, your husband sure doesn't know what he's doing!'

It's not just derogatory statements you're on the alert for, it's derogatory communication and a gesture is very definitely a communication.

Finding a correct "third party," someone who has actually been promoting conflict, can bring tremendous relief to a relationship. It can also bring two people a lot closer together!

This is a very exact tool. Use it exactly the way it is laid out and you will be delighted with the results!

[Note: You don't have to go through a Third Party Investigation to benefit from this chapter. An important lesson here is not to allow someone to unreasonably criticize your mate. Just stop the person dead in their tracks before they launch into some derogatory comment or lecture. Be known in your circles as the type of person who does NOT allow that kind of communication. The affinity that you have with your mate will be strengthened by this… and this very same affinity will be weakened when you allow others to make derogatory comments. Just don't allow it.]

Chapter Six
COOLING THINGS OFF

The first two chapters give two tools to repair a relationship. They work. They work splendidly.

But what if you and your partner have just recently had a fight and you're both too upset to write up your overts and withholds or sit through a Third Party investigation?

Mr. Hubbard developed a technique known as an 'assist'. An assist is *"an action which can be done to alleviate a present time discomfort and help a person recover more rapidly from an accident, illness or upset"*.

One type of an assist that you can do is very, very simple ... but very powerful. From the works of Mr. Hubbard:

> *"If one feels antagonistic toward one's wife, the right thing to do is to go out and take a walk around the block until one feels better, and make her walk around the block in the opposite direction until an extroversion* from the situation is achieved."*

While you are both out taking this walk, put your attention on the physical things around you. Notice the houses, trees, clouds—put your attention *outwards*. This will help you to accomplish an "extroversion", which is simply having one's attention outwards.

Here is another assist that can be done to help the two of you. Once again from the materials of Mr. Hubbard:

> *"When marital tensions have been left unaddressed and unhandled for some time, they can break out with violence. Severe fights can cause quite an emotional upset for either or both partners, and the threat of loss occasioned by such quarrels can be profound."*

"Where a fight has occurred between marital partners, the following assist can be used to help handle any resultant emotional trauma* of husband and/or wife.

"This assist may be done by marital partners on each other after a fight or may be used by another person to help one or both partners."

"Procedure

"1. Tell the person you are going to help them get over any adverse emotional reaction to the fight.

"2. Have the person sit down in a comfortable chair across from you.

"3. Say to the person, 'Give me places where an angry (husband/wife) would be safe.' For example, if you were doing this on a wife, you would say, 'Give me places where an angry husband would be safe.'

"4. Get an answer from the person and acknowledge their answer, with a 'Thank you,' or 'Good,' etc.

"5. Then say to the person, 'Give me places where an angry (husband/wife) would find you safe.'

"6. Get an answer and acknowledge it.

"7. Repeat steps 3-6 over and over again until the person is happy again and has had a realization* of some kind—about himself, his spouse, the situation or just life in general.

"When this occurs, tell the person 'End of Assist.'

"Be certain not to evaluate* the person's answers for him or tell him how he should answer or what he should think about the situation. Do not berate the person for his answers. This is destructive and can halt all potential gain from the assist.

"This assist is not a handling for the situation which caused the conflict or discord. Once the immediate upset is under control, the reasons for the fight should be ascertained*. For instance, another party such as a relative or associate of a spouse may be creating friction between the marital partners. When this third party, usually hidden, is exposed as the source of the conflict, it resolves."

It is probably easiest (and safest) to have this procedure done by someone besides you or your partner. You and your partner *can* do this procedure on each other, but someone outside of the relationship is usually in a better frame of mind to carry it out.

For the person who will be administering* this assist, here are a few points to keep in mind:

- Whatever answers the person gives each time should simply be acknowledged. Do not discuss any of the answers. Don't give your opinion about any answer — just simply acknowledge each answer (by saying, "Thank you", "Good", "Great", etc.)

- If this process is run correctly, the person will feel better at the end and will have a realization of some kind at the end of the process. Do not continue the assist past this point.

- Be sure to run this process on both partners.

What you have here is an exact procedure. Don't vary it, don't alter it even slightly, don't invent a few twists of your own— just apply it exactly the way it's written and you will have a very good result.

Chapter Seven

COMMUNICATION

You've certainly heard all about the importance of communication. If your relationship is not in great shape, you may have even endured (or given) several lectures about communication.

After writing up your overts and withholds and if a Third Party needed to be found (chapters 3 and 4), you will find the willingness to communicate has gone up significantly. Now we need to keep it going up. To quote Mr. Hubbard:

> *"One's ability to communicate can spell the difference between success and failure in all aspects of living. You will notice that those people you know who are successful in their endeavors generally have a high ability to communicate; those who are not, do not.*
>
> *"Communication is not just a way of getting along in life, it is the heart of life. It is by thousands of percent the senior factor in understanding life and living it successfully."*
>
> *"In examining the whole subject of communication, one is apt to discover, if he takes a penetrating look, that there are very few people around him who are actually* communicating, *but that there are a lot of people who think they are communicating who are not.*
>
> *"The apparency* sometimes is that it is better not to communicate than to communicate, but that is never the case. Communication is the solvent* for any human problem.*

First let's look at the key parts that make up communication. Mr. Hubbard says:

> *"The formula of communication is cause, distance, effect, with intention, attention and duplication with understanding."*

I do not want this to get technical, but it's important to have a clear understanding of each of the terms. Then we will see how they all fit together and how it can improve a relationship.

CAUSE

For our purposes, cause simply means the originator of the communication, the person who sends the communication.

DISTANCE

The distance is the space between the originator of the communication and the person(s) receiving it.

Distance? That sounds simple enough. But sometimes we don't take into consideration the actual distance and our communication falls short.

EFFECT

This is the receipt point of the communication. For our purposes, the person (or persons) receiving the communication.

INTENTION

Intention is the *want* or *desire* to accomplish something. Your intention to do something is your want or desire to get that something done. If you have a very weak intention to wake up in the morning, then you'll probably roll over in bed and catch a few more winks. If you have an extremely strong intention to get home in time to watch one of your favorite shows, then you may exceed the speed limit to make that happen.

Intention. It's your desire or want to accomplish something.

In terms of communication, intention is very, very important.

First of all, there is the distance between CAUSE and EFFECT. The originator of the communication needs to have sufficient intention to get the communication across that distance.

The originator also needs to have sufficient intention that the receipt point actually receives the communication! This is not just about loudness. This is a specific intention: the intention that the receipt point receives the communication.

While all of this is happening at the originating point, what is happening at the receipt point?

ATTENTION

The person receiving the communication has to give attention to the person sending the communication.

This seems very obvious, doesn't it? But this is where many communications fall apart. This is where many communications don't even qualify as communication.

How many times have you said something to somebody who wasn't really paying attention? What was the result? You either had to clarify what you said or repeat what you said. Maybe you had to repeat yourself several times. This can be frustrating, even quite irritating!

The person may even be looking at you straight in the eye and yet NOT paying attention, or not paying enough attention. It doesn't matter if the person is looking at you, what matters is the ATTENTION. If the person is not paying adequate attention to you, he/she will not get the full communication. In fact, communication has not yet occurred.

Attention is very important to proper communication.

How else could attention be lacking?

Have you ever been in a conversation and you were thinking about something else? Your attention is elsewhere, and therefore you don't get the full communication that is coming your way.

Have you ever been in a conversation and halfway through the message that is coming your way, you are already thinking about your response? Guess what? Your attention on the originator and his/her message has just been significantly reduced, and so has the quality of the communication!

Sometimes people are "dwelling in the past." They are not fully in present time. To the degree that this is happening, to that degree one's attention is not fully available for present time communication.

When you give the person communicating your full attention, you will find communication has been dramatically improved. And when both parties give each other full attention, then we truly have a much better scene.

There are two reasons why you want to give full attention to what is being said to you. The first is:

DUPLICATION

Duplication is the act of making an exact copy of something. Did you know that copy machines were once called "duplicators"? They made exact copies of the original.

In communication, the person receiving the communication makes an exact copy of what came from the originator.

If the receiving person does not make an exact copy of what came across that distance, then communication does not occur. Something different happens. And more times than not, that something different gets us into some difficulty.

If Person A says to Person B:

"I'm not really upset with you, I just don't understand why you came home so late."

Now, Person B might not exactly duplicate that communication and instead the "copy" that was made at Person B was:

"I'm really upset with you, I don't understand why you came home so late."

So of course, we have trouble brewing. This trouble could've been completely avoided if Person B had exactly duplicated what Person A had communicated.

If this exchange of "communication" caused an upset, who would have been responsible for this upset?

Tick tock.

Tick tock.

Both Person A and B!

Why? Because Person A should have used the proper amount of INTENTION necessary so that Person B received an exact DUPLICATION of what Person A sent!

And Person B should have used the correct amount of ATTENTION so that he/she was able to make a full DUPLICATION of what came across.

Attention also plays a part for Person A, the originator. The person sending the communication has to have attention on the person receiving the communication. This is often taken for granted, but how many times do you recall somebody saying something to you but not really paying full attention to you?

And intention is important for Person B, the receipt point. Person B needs to have good intention to receive and duplicate what is coming across the distance. If Person B's intention is weak, he/she may not get fully what was said. Have you ever talked to someone whose intention to listen to you was not really there? What kind of conversation was that?

Yes, yes, yes, we've always known that communication is a two-way street. But now we are finding out what ingredients each person uses to ensure that communication works. These ingredients may seem simple. But simple things can produce very powerful results.

What is the purpose of Person A's intention and attention and Person B's attention and duplication?

UNDERSTANDING

The whole purpose is to create understanding. And if each of the ingredients above is IN, that is exactly what will occur.

How important is it for you and your partner to better understand each other?

Let's take a look at a few examples of communication and let's see what happens when these key ingredients are not fully in use.

> Mary is going over the family finances and wants to tell Bill that they are overdue on one of their credit cards. Bill is underneath the sink working on a leak. Mary does not use adequate INTENTION to ensure that Bill's ATTENTION is really present.
>
> Mary says, "Bill, the Visa card is overdue and we need to get a payment to them." Bill doesn't quite hear her and is straining to get his pliers around the pipe that is leaking. So he responds, "Okay, Mary!"
>
> Mary comes away from this "conversation" feeling that she has alerted Bill to the matter and that he will get a payment off to the credit card company.

> Several weeks later, Bill storms into the living room, "Mary, why didn't you tell me about this overdue credit card?!"
>
> Mary feels a bit betrayed and says, "I did! A couple of weeks ago ... I'm sure I did."
>
> Bill responds, "There's no need to stretch the truth on this Mary. I'm certain you never told me about this!"

It's very obvious what should've happened here. Before Mary told Bill about the overdue credit card, she should've ensured that she had Bill's ATTENTION. Mary needed to use a bit more INTENTION to make this happen. Bill, on his end, did not have a very good DUPLICATION of what Mary said, and the end result was a MISUNDERSTANDING.

Yes, this example of Bill being under the sink is a very obvious example of how important it is to get someone's attention first before communicating.

But there are many, many instances where it is not so obvious yet the outcome is very similar to the one above. Here is another example:

> Let's say Mary and Bill have just had an upset. Bill has somewhat gotten over this upset, but Mary is still seething inside. Bill, not recognizing this, says to Mary, "don't forget the dinner at Bennigan's tomorrow night with the Oglethorpes!"
>
> Mary, still embroiled* over the fight, did not have her full attention available for what Bill said and the "duplication" she made of the message was: "don't forget the dinner at Bennihanna's tomorrow night with the Oglethorpes."
>
> And guess where Mary shows up for dinner?
>
> Mary "heard" Bennihanna's even though Bill said Bennigan's. Communication did not occur.
>
> Bill did not have enough ATTENTION on Mary to observe that her ATTENTION was not sufficiently present. He sort of suspected this, but the bottom line was he didn't use enough INTENTION to make sure he really had her ATTENTION. Not having her full attention caused a misDUPLICATION of what was said and the net result was another upset.
>
> Let's look at another example:

Mary hasn't told Bill recently how she feels about him, so she runs right up to him and says, "Bill, you know I really love you." The exact words "you know I really love you" remind Bill unconsciously of a time when a woman said that to him just before she broke off the relationship.

Bill responds with a tone of disbelief, "Yes, I'm sure you do."

Mary has no idea what has caused Bill to react this way. She tries several times to get Bill to tell her what's wrong, but he just shrugs it off and walks away.

What has happened here? This is a very subtle, but very real, example of how DUPLICATION was missing. What Bill unfortunately "duplicated" was something that occurred to him in the past. He did not DUPLICATE (make an exact copy of) what Mary said to him in present time. He did not "get" what Mary said. What he "got" was something that another woman (from his past) said. It doesn't matter how subtle this can get, the rules of communication are the same.

Cut Communications

Have you ever said something to somebody and before you finished what you were saying, the person cuts you off and says something back? If I had a nickel for every time that happened on this planet, I would retire and buy a few continents!

When this kind of thing happens (cutting the communication line) several things happen:

We're certain that Person B has not fully duplicated what Person A has said.

We're certain that Person A's attention is not fully available for Person B's new communication because Person A is in the middle of communicating something.

Neither Person A or Person B are communicating fully.

There are a number of things that can happen that make communication less effective than it should be. Not enough INTENTION, inadequate ATTENTION, a poor DUPLICATION of what came across, little to no UNDERSTANDING.

Each time communication does not occur the way it should, an upset occurs. It may just be a tiny upset, but it is an upset nonetheless. When a relationship accumulates enough of these "tiny" (or not so tiny) upsets, eventually we experience major upsets.

Take some time during the day and observe others communicating. Notice the different parts of communication at work (or not at work). Observe how much real attention people give to each other while communicating.

Observe the intention that people use to get a communication across. Observe what happens when good intention is used and also observe what happens when weak intention is employed. Notice the difference in the outcome of the communication.

While you are observing others communicate, notice how good or bad their duplication is. Do you notice that when certain people duplicate very well, that others really enjoy communicating and being with them?

Look closely at how others communicate. First look intently at the individual parts of communication: attention, intention and duplication.

After looking at these individual components of communication, now take a close look at people who use these three components very well. Can you see how well they understand each other?

If each of the parts of communication are known and used, even the smallest upsets can be prevented. And when you get more and more familiar with these tools, you will see your relationship improving on a daily basis.

Chapter Eight

COMMUNICATION'S TWO BEST FRIENDS

When you start off a conversation with someone you've never met before, what do you instinctively do? You find something that the two of you have in common, right? And then you try to talk about that for a little while.

When you talk about something that you both have in common, it's easier to communicate with each other, yes? You have found a common point of reality.

Mr. Hubbard defines the word **reality** as: "*that which appears to be. Reality is fundamentally agreement. What we agree to be real is real*".

Let's say you and a friend are at an art museum and you're both standing in front of a painting. Your friend says, "Boy, that's really beautiful!" You look at the same painting and you think, 'Boy, that's really weird!' You may end up saying something different to your friend, but your viewpoint of the painting is that it's weird.

Your reality is different than your friend's reality. Maybe if the two of you talked for a half an hour about your different viewpoints of the painting, maybe your friend might see the "weirdness" of the painting that you see and maybe you would see some of the "beauty" that your friend saw. If that occurs, then both of your realities would have shifted or changed somewhat.

You both agree that what you are looking at is a painting. That reality is very easily agreed to. Beyond that point, we do not have the same point of agreement and therefore the realities are different.

Taken to the extreme, you could have a person in very bad mental shape who looks at a table in front of him and instead of seeing a table he sees something very threatening; perhaps the table appears to him to be a buzzsaw. His reality doesn't come close to what many others agree to: that there is simply a table there. So this mentally unbalanced individual has difficulties with reality, even things as obvious as a table.

The subject of reality is very important to our efforts to improve communication with others.

Take a second now and consider the different things that are very real to your partner. How recently have you talked about these things?

The more you communicate to others about things that are REAL to them, the easier it will be to communicate and the more affinity there will be.

Affinity is defined as: the degree of liking.

If you have a great deal of affinity for someone or something, your degree of liking is high. You could also have very little affinity for someone — you don't like that person very much at all.

L. Ron Hubbard discovered that affinity, reality and communication actually form a triangle:

This triangle is called the ARC Triangle.

A for Affinity

R for Reality

C for Communication

Mr. Hubbard said:

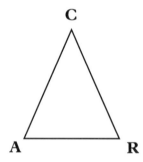

> "Every point on the ARC triangle is dependent on the other two, and every two are dependent on one. One can't cut down one without cutting down the other two, and one can't rehabilitate* one without rehabilitating the other two. On the positive side, one can rehabilitate any point on the triangle by rehabilitating any other point on it.
>
> "The interrelationship* of the triangle becomes apparent at once when one asks, 'Have you ever tried to talk to an angry man?' Without a high degree of liking and without some basis of agreement there is no communication. Without communication and some basis of emotional response there can be no reality. Without some basis for agreement and communication there can be no affinity. Thus we call these three things a triangle. Unless we have two corners of a triangle, there cannot be a third corner. Desiring any corner of the triangle, one must include the other two.

> *"The triangle is not an equilateral* triangle. Affinity and reality are very much less important than communication. It might be said that the triangle begins with communication, which brings into existence affinity and reality.*
>
> *"Since each of these three aspects of existence is dependent on the other two, anything which affects one of these will also similarly affect the others. It is very difficult to suffer a reversal of affinity without also suffering a blockage of communication and a consequent deterioration of reality."*

Let's go over these points a bit more. When one corner of the triangle lowers, the other two corners lower as well.

When you are talking to a really close friend, and your friend tells you something that you are in thorough disagreement with, you can actually notice, for that brief moment in time, a lessening in affinity for your very close friend. You will also notice a lessening in the desire to communicate. Because the relationship with your close friend is sufficiently solid, you keep at it and resolve your differences. But the principle of this triangle did manifest itself. When the reality went down, so did the other two corners of the triangle: affinity and communication.

When you meet up with someone you have virtually no affinity for, you do not really want to communicate with this person. You believe there's very little that the two of you have in common. If you did manage to have a conversation and you both talked about a few minor things that you each had good reality on (agreed with), you would find the willingness to communicate increasing and, yes, you would notice an increase (even if slight) in the level of affinity.

This triangle may seem very simple. It is. It is also a very powerful tool that will help you start, maintain and repair all the important relationships of your life.

If you and your loved one have experienced a lessening of affinity, what should you do? Well, very definitely the communication point of the triangle should be addressed. That makes sense. But what should you talk about? How about things that your mate has a good deal of reality on? If you communicate to your partner on subjects that he/she has good reality on (agrees with) you will find it a lot easier to get into communication with your partner. If you keep at it for a little while, you will find your partner's willingness to communicate with you will increase and his/her affinity for you will also go up.

Even when you're having the most pressing problems, you might just do what the last paragraph suggests and do nothing else. In other words, if you just communicate on subjects that your partner has excellent reality on, and you do that over a period of a few days or so, you will see affinity increase. And, you will have produced a greater willingness in your partner to discuss some of the more pressing problems.

You could discuss life's problems while the two of you are very out of communication with each other and not having a great deal of affinity for each other or you could have the same discussion when both of you are in much better communication with each other. Which approach would you prefer?

Practical Exercises

The following exercises will help you understand the ARC Triangle better and increase your ability to apply it. They are excerpted from a workbook of Mr. Hubbard's:

1) Look around the environment and spot* ten instances where an individual is displaying affinity.

2) Look around the environment and spot ten examples where two or more individuals have reality on something.

3) Look around the environment and spot ten examples of communication.

4) Spot more examples of affinity, reality and communication, noticing how they interrelate. Continue to spot examples of affinity, reality and communication as above until you clearly see the relationship between these and are sure that each depends on the other two.

5) Using the data you have learned about the ARC triangle, raise the reality between yourself and another person. Establish reality by finding something with which you and the other person agree. Repeat this with different people as many times as needed until you can raise reality between yourself and another with ease.

6) Using the data you have learned about the ARC triangle, increase the affinity between yourself and another person. Find something you can like about the person, and note the difference in affinity you have for the person as a result. Repeat this with different people as many times as needed until you can raise affinity between yourself and another with ease.

7) Using the data you have learned about the ARC triangle, raise the communication level between yourself and another person. Repeat this with other people, over and over, until you are confident you can raise the communication level between yourself and others.

8) Using the data you have learned about the ARC triangle, raise the ARC between yourself and another person. Repeat this with other people, over and over, until you are confident you can raise ARC between yourself and others.

The ARC Triangle is a superb tool to improve relationships. Use it often!

Chapter Nine

PUTTING ORDER INTO YOUR RELATIONSHIPS

This chapter will give you a whole new perspective on how to put order into your life and into your important relationships.

When things are running smoothly and people are working well together and getting things accomplished, you can say "order" exists. When things are not running smoothly and people are not working very well together, then we have disorder.

One sees all kinds of disorder in life. But many people try to handle the disorder directly. This approach does not work.

Here is an excellent quote from Mr. Hubbard on this subject:

> *"When you start to introduce order into anything, disorder shows up and blows off*. Therefore, efforts to bring order in the society or any part of it will be productive of disorder for a short while every time.*
>
> *"The trick is to keep on bringing order and soon the disorder is gone and you have orderly activity remaining. But if you* hate *disorder and fight disorder only, don't ever try to bring order to anything, for the resulting disorder will drive you half mad.*
>
> *"Only if you can ignore disorder and can understand this principle can you have a working world."*

Let's take a look at this more closely.

When you start to bring order into anything, disorder shows up and then blows off (disappears). What happens with some of us, however, is this: we attempt to put some order into an activity and some disorder shows up. We become upset or agitated by this disorder and we stop putting order in. We either try to handle the disorder directly, or we go off to some other area where this disorder is not visible or we go for a nice walk to calm ourselves down.

But what if you KNEW ahead of time that your attempts to put order into an activity would be productive of disorder? What if you were very certain of that? You would not be so inclined to be thrown off by the disorder that surfaces. You would know ahead of time that disorder was going to show up and knowing that would put you in a much, much better position to deal with the resulting disorder.

And how should you deal with the resulting disorder? By putting in more order. Mr. Hubbard says: "*The trick is to keep on bringing order; and soon the disorder is gone, and you have orderly activity remaining.*"

Now that doesn't mean that while you are putting order into your relationship with your husband, if the fire alarm rings and smoke is pouring out of the back office, that you ignore the smoke and keep on putting in order. Don't go robotic on this. The focus is on continuing to put order in. If you keep on putting order in, the disorder WILL finally blow off (disappear) and yes, you will have orderly activity remaining.

This next point is VERY important:

As you apply the different principles throughout this book, you will be putting order into your life and into your relationships. This process will be productive of some disorder. This disorder could show up in many different forms: you could get flustered; you could get upset; your partner could get aggravated or angry; a relative may come over and cause a dispute; all kinds of different things could happen.

Realize this: disorder is surfacing. Ignore it and keep on putting in the order. Keep on applying the principles in this book and the disorder will eventually disappear and you will have a much better scene.

For example, let's say you are in the middle of doing an O/W Write-up that is explained in detail in Chapter Four. During this write-up, your husband calls and says he'll be home late. You might get upset at this point and be tempted to say something derogatory back to your husband. Or you could step back for a second and realize that you are putting some order into your life by doing this O/W Write-up and instead of getting flustered by the disorder that surfaces, you acknowledge your husband and keep right on doing the O/W Write-up. In other words, you keep on putting the order into the scene.

This technology on order and disorder may seem very, very simple. But it is very powerful. If you know ahead of time that attempts on your part to put in order will be productive of disorder every time, and if you then just continue to put in the order—the disorder will be history.

Keep on putting in order and your relationships and your life will move along more smoothly and much more to your satisfaction!

Chapter Ten
FREEING YOURSELF FROM THE PAST

The past has a knack* of affecting us in the present and also reducing our ability to create the future. This can be especially true with relationships.

What if you recently separated from or divorced your husband or wife? What if you just broke up with your boyfriend? What if you are still experiencing unpleasant emotions about this?

What if you broke up with someone ten years ago and you're still not over it?

The upset caused by an ended relationship can sometimes be quite severe.

Fortunately there are several procedures you can use to free up your attention from these past relationships. This chapter will present two of them. If you do both of these procedures fully and correctly, you will experience a great deal of relief. You will be able to operate more freely in the present and you will increase your ability to create the future.

The first procedure is an assist. If you recall from the Chapter "Cooling Things Off," Mr. Hubbard defines an assist as *"an action which can be done to alleviate a present time discomfort and help a person recover more rapidly from an accident, illness or upset"*.

With this assist, you will need the help of someone. Choose a person that you have a good relationship with and who easily accepts your communication.

This person is going to ask you a specific question over and over again. Each time this question is asked, you give an answer. This procedure is continued until you feel much better. This will be accompanied by some kind of realization or new thought about yourself, the situation, or life in general. It is important that the procedure be continued until you feel much better.

The question that is asked is:

"Find something that isn't reminding you of _____ (that person)."

So, if you are still experiencing some upset concerning a break-up with John, the person helping you would say:

"Find something that isn't reminding you of John."

You would then carry out that request and tell the person what it is that isn't reminding you of John.

The person running the procedure on you would then acknowledge what you said by saying:

"Okay."

"Thanks."

"Good."

"Thank you." ... anything that serves as an acknowledgment. In other words, each time you find something that isn't reminding you of John and you tell the person what it is, the person gives you an acknowledgment of some kind.

Here is an example of how this might run:

Sue just broke up with Steve (or Sue broke up with Steve years ago but is still experiencing upset about it).

Sue's friend Mary comes over to run the above procedure. Sue and Mary both read this entire chapter so they both know how the procedure works and then Mary starts it off:

Mary: "Find something that isn't reminding you of John."

Sue: "Yes, this room over here. He never goes in there."

Mary: "Thank you. Find something that isn't reminding you of John."

Sue: "Well, this book I've been reading."

Mary: "Great. Find something that isn't reminding you of John."

Sue: "Uh, well, this spoon doesn't remind me of John."

Mary: "Very good. Find something that isn't reminding you of John."

Sue: "Hmm. I'm having a hard time finding anything else."

Mary: "I understand. Let me give you the question again: Find something that isn't reminding you of John."

Sue: "Okay, I'll keep at it. Well, this mirror doesn't remind me of John."

Mary: "Excellent. Find something that isn't reminding you of John."

Sue: "My shoes don't remind me of John."

Mary: "Thank you. Find something that isn't reminding you of John."

Sue: "The waste basket over there definitely does not remind me of John. He never threw things away!"

Mary: "Okay. Find something that isn't reminding you of John."

Sue: "Well, the window."

Mary: "Great. Find something that isn't reminding you of John."

Sue: "Hey, how long do we have to do this!?"

Mary: "Well, let's continue, Sue, and see how it goes. Find something that isn't reminding you of John."

Sue: "Okay, let's see. Oh, that door definitely does remind me of John. (Sue starts crying) I remember him walking out on me!

Mary: "Okay. Here's the question again: Find something that isn't reminding you of John."

Sue: (crying stops) "Well, my pencil sharpener does not remind me of John!"

Mary: "Real good. Find something that isn't reminding you of John."

Sue: "The new throw rug over by the closet doesn't remind me of John."

Mary: "Okay. Find something that isn't reminding you of John."

Sue: "You know, I feel a lot better about this. I realize that I don't have to have my life revolve completely around another person! Hey, that was nice."

That was an example of how it might go. This procedure could go much longer or it could even complete itself faster than the example above. Keep at it until the person feels better about things.

As noted in an earlier chapter, the person administering this assist should keep these points in mind:

- Whatever answers the person gives each time should simply be acknowledged. Don't discuss any of the answers. Don't give your opinion about any answer—just simply acknowledge each answer (by saying, "Thank you", "Good," "Great" etc.)

- If this process is run correctly, the person will feel better at the end and should have a realization of some kind at the end of the process. Do not continue the assist past this point.

- Once again, what you have here is an exact procedure. Don't vary it, don't alter it even slightly, don't invent a few twists of your own — just apply it exactly the way it's written and you will have a very good result.

The next procedure will significantly help free up your attention from the past. If you have suffered a broken relationship of any kind and are still experiencing upset from this, then apply this next procedure. Your upset from an earlier relationship can take many forms. If you feel angry, hurt, critical, griefy, or any unpleasant emotion associated with the person you broke up with, this procedure will help you significantly.

This procedure was discussed in great detail in Chapter Four: writing up one's overts and withholds (O/Ws). If you are the least bit uncertain about how to write up your O/Ws, go back to Chapter Four and thoroughly review the material. Briefly, Mr. Hubbard points out:

> *"A harmful act or a transgression against the moral code of a group is called an* overt act. *When a person does something that is contrary to the moral code he has agreed to, or when he omits to do something that he should have done per that moral code, he has committed an overt act. An overt act violates what was agreed upon.*
>
> *"An unspoken, unannounced transgression against a moral code by which the person is bound is called a* withhold. *A withhold is an overt act a person committed that he or she is not talking about. It is something a person believes that, if revealed, will endanger his self-preservation. Any withhold comes* after *an overt act.*
>
> *"Thus, an overt act is something done; a withhold is an overt act withheld from another or others."*

You and your partner had a moral code together. It might've been unspoken, you may not have sat down and hammered out this moral code, but you did have a set of agreements as to what was right and what was wrong.

At one time or another we do things that go against these agreements. These are overts. We may have omitted to do some things that we know we should have done.

These omissions are overts. And when we then withhold these different things from our partner, we have withholds.

If you are experiencing any upset or unpleasant emotion connected to a break-up with someone, you will derive tremendous relief if you sit down and do a thorough O/W Write-up.

Yes, I realize that you may feel hurt by what the other person has done to you. Yes, I understand that you may consider the other person didn't treat you right. I understand all of this. But, what will give you the greatest relief is discovering in this O/W Write-up what you have done or omitted to do.

Trust me on this. If you follow this procedure exactly, you will experience major relief.

Sit down, get a pad of paper and a pen or pencil. For those with a computer, open up your word processor*. Start the process of writing up your overts and withholds in relation to this other person.

You may have done something before your relationship with John that you didn't tell John about, that you always wondered if you should have told him. Fair enough, write that up as a withhold.

Here are some examples of O/Ws that Sue might write up in relation to John:

1. I lied to John about our vacation tickets.

2. About 2 years ago, it was my job to purchase the vacation tickets. I knew they had to be purchased two weeks in advance to get the discount. I forgot to do this and when John got home, I sat down with him in the living room and told him that the travel agent had messed up the flight arrangements. This was a lie. I also told him the travel agent gave us a discount for having "messed up"— this also was a lie. John looked at me and accepted my explanation. I never told him that I had omitted to handle the advance purchase, and that I had lied to him.

1. I flirted with John's boss and even let him kiss me.

2. John's boss came over to the house about a year and a half ago and wanted to speak with me. At first, I didn't know what it was all about, but it soon became apparent he wanted to flirt with me, perhaps more. I then flirted back with him, saying flirty things to him that egged him on. He came over to me on the couch and kissed me on the cheek and was about to kiss me on the lips when I stopped it and told him we shouldn't be doing this. He reluctantly agreed and left. I never told John that this happened.

1. I aborted a child prior to my going out with John.

2. About 3 years before I started dating John, I got pregnant with someone who had no interest in a long term relationship. I didn't tell a soul about this, but I went off and had the child aborted. I had the abortion in a town about 100 miles north of my home town. When I first got together with John, we talked about all kinds of things. I remember one time at Tom and Eddy's diner, we talked about abortion. I told him I was totally against this and would never contemplate doing it. This was a lie, as I had my own child aborted some three years before.

1. I took a ten dollar bill from John's wallet and didn't tell him even when he asked about it.

2. This was just a few weeks before we broke up. It was no big deal that I took the $10 from his wallet, the big deal was that I didn't tell him when he asked about it. His wallet was on the chest of drawers in the dining room and he was upstairs working at the computer. I wanted to get some Chinese food but I was short on cash. I took the ten dollar bill and for some stupid reason, when he asked "hey, do you know what happened to the cash in my wallet?" — I said, "No."

The above are examples of overts and withholds that Sue might write up. How many of these should be written up? There is no set number to write up. You continue writing until you are satisfied they are complete. You will feel very good about it, and you will experience relief. Do not carry on with this procedure beyond this point.

IMPORTANT NOTE: If you are the least bit uncertain on how to write up your O/Ws, go back and thoroughly review Chapter Four. It is very important that you understand the theory behind this procedure as well as the procedure itself.

If you feel you are bogging down during the write-up, you should take a short break. During this break take a walk outside and look at the many physical objects around you: trees, cars, sky, etc. Actually place your attention on the things outside of you. This will help. Then get back in there and continue the write-up.

If, after taking a walk, the write-up is still not going well, go back and restudy Chapter Four. Reread the section explaining overts, withholds, justifications and the procedure on writing up O/Ws. Make sure you are following the procedure exactly. If you have not been writing up each overt or withhold exactly the way it is laid out, then go through your write-up and correct any overts or withholds that you have not written up correctly.

Do not leave this write-up incomplete. Do a thorough write-up and you will be very satisfied with how you feel.

The above two procedures can be of significant benefit to you if you are still experiencing sadness or anger or any other unpleasant emotion associated with an earlier relationship. It does not matter if the relationship ended last week or 15 years ago. If you are still upset about it, then use one or both procedures above and you will feel much, much better.

Chapter Eleven

CHOOSING YOUR PEOPLE

Choosing your friends and of course choosing a lifetime mate—these are important decisions. Sometimes we make these decisions with very limited information. In the case of a lifelong partner, a wrong decision can be disastrous.

When it comes to choosing our mates, what do we really know about them? When the courting period is over, how will our partner handle the various circumstances of life? How will they will handle responsibility? How truthful will they be? Do we know how this person will really treat children? A few months down the line, how much respect will this person show for you, for your friends, for your family?

Before we start a meaningful relationship, what should we know about our new partner-to-be? Is it possible to know how they will handle the components of life and a relationship?

Yes, and with the help of two powerful tools, you will be able to predict and understand the people you live your life with.

These two tools will also make it a lot easier for you when choosing new people to live and work with.

The first tool is "The Emotional Tone Scale". From the works of Mr. Hubbard:

> *"The Tone Scale—a vital tool for any aspect of life involving one's fellows—is a scale which shows the successive emotional tones a person can experience. By 'tone' is meant the momentary or continuing emotional state of a person. Emotions such as fear, anger, grief, enthusiasm and others which people experience are shown on this graduated scale.*
>
> *"Skillful use of this scale enables one to both predict and understand human behavior in all its manifestations.*

"*This Tone Scale plots the descending spiral of life from full vitality* and consciousness* through half-vitality and half-consciousness down to death.*

"*By various calculations about the energy of life, by observation and by test, this Tone Scale is able to give levels of behavior as life declines.*

"*These various levels are common to all people.*

"*When a man is nearly dead, he can be said to be in a chronic** **apathy**. *And he behaves a certain way about other things. This is 0.05 on the Tone Scale.*

"*When a man is chronically in* **grief** *about his losses, he is in grief. And he behaves certain ways about many things. This is 0.5 on the scale.*

"*When a person is not yet so low as grief but realizes his losses are impending*, or is fixed chronically at this level by past losses, he can be said to be in* **fear**. *This is around 1.0 on the scale.*

"*An individual who is fighting against threatened losses is in* **anger**. *And he manifests other aspects of behavior. This is 1.5.*

"*The person who is merely suspicious that loss may take place or who has become fixed at this level is resentful. He can be said to be in* **antagonism**. *This is 2.0 on the scale.*

"*Above antagonism, the situation of a person is not so good that he is enthusiastic, not so bad that he is resentful. He has lost some goals and cannot immediately locate others. He is said to be in* **boredom**, *or at 2.5 on the Tone Scale.*

"*At 3.0 on the scale, the person has a* **conservative**, *cautious aspect towards life but is reaching his goals.*

"*At 4.0 the individual is* **enthusiastic**, *happy and vital.*

"*Very few people are natural 4.0s. A charitable average is probably around 2.8.*

"*You have watched this scale in operation before now. Have you ever seen a child trying to acquire, let us say, a nickel? At first he is happy. He simply wants a nickel. If refused, he then explains why he wants it. If he fails to get it and did not want it badly, he becomes bored and goes away. But if he wants it badly, he will get antagonistic about it. Then he will become angry. Then, that failing, he may lie about why he wants it. That failing, he goes into grief. And if he is still refused, he finally sinks into apathy and says he doesn't want it. This is negation.*

"A child threatened by danger also dwindles down the scale. At first he does not appreciate that danger is posed at him and he is quite cheerful. Then the danger, let us say it is a dog, starts to approach him. The child sees the danger but still does not believe it is for him and keeps on with his business. But his playthings 'bore' him for the moment. He is a little apprehensive and not sure. Then the dog comes nearer. The child 'resents him' or shows some antagonism. The dog comes nearer still. The child becomes angry and makes some effort to injure the dog. The dog comes still nearer and is more threatening. The child becomes afraid. Fear unavailing, the child cries. If the dog still threatens him, the child may go into an apathy and simply wait to be bitten.

"Objects or animals or people which assist survival, as they become inaccessible* to the individual, bring him down the Tone Scale.

"Objects, animals or people which threaten survival, as they approach the individual, bring him down the Tone Scale.

"This scale has a chronic or an acute* aspect. A person can be brought down the Tone Scale to a low level for ten minutes and then go back up, or he can be brought down it for ten years and not go back up.

"A man who has suffered too many losses, too much pain, tends to become fixed at some lower level of the scale and, with only slight fluctuations, stays there. Then his general and common behavior will be at that level of the Tone Scale."

The next chapter gives The Emotional Tone Scale. Each tone is then further described using data from Mr. Hubbard's works.

Chapter Twelve
THE EMOTIONAL TONE SCALE

By L. Ron Hubbard

4.0	Enthusiasm
3.5	Strong Interest
3.0	Conservatism
2.5	Boredom
2.0	Antagonism
1.5	Anger
1.1	Covert Hostility
1.0	Fear
0.5	Grief
0.05	Apathy

From Mr. Hubbard's works, here is more information on each tone.

0.05 Apathy

"At apathy, a person will give the appearance of looking fixedly* for minutes on end, at a particular object. Only thing is, he doesn't see it. He isn't aware of the object at all. If you dropped a bag over his head, the focus of his eyes would probably remain the same.

"Affinity at this level is expressed by complete withdrawal from people. There is, in apathy, no real attempt to contact one's self and no attempt to contact others. The apathy case will try to discourage anyone from doing anything. Hopes and dreams are destroyed merely be claiming that they are hopeless and impossible.

"Apathy is more than hopeless: it is death in a very forthright form. The apathy case talks about death, threatens personal death, and will actually attempt suicide."

0.5 Grief

"Moving up to grief, the person looks 'downcast'. A person in chronic grief tends to focus his eyes down in the direction of the floor a good bit. In the lower ranges of grief, his attention will be fairly fixed, as in apathy.

"Here we have pleas for pity, desperate efforts to win support by tears. This takes place where one recognizes his loss and failure as in the death of somebody he loved and tried to help. The person in grief talks dolefully* and hopelessly in terms of bad things which are happening and will happen and for which there is no remedy. He listens only to such conversation. He cannot be heartened or cheered up."

1.0 Fear

"As a person starts moving up into the fear band, you get the focus shifting around, but still directed downward. At fear itself, the very obvious characteristic is that the person can't look at you. People are too dangerous to look at. He's supposedly talking to you, but he's looking over in left field. Then he glances at your feet briefly, then over your head (you get the impression a plane's passing over) but now he's looking back over his shoulder. Flick, flick, flick. In short, he'll look anywhere but at you.

"In this tone, the affinity is poor, being fearful, the communication is twisted and consists of lies, the reality is poor and is agreed upon for covert* purposes.

"Fear is expressed on its highest level as acute shyness, stage fright, extreme modesty, being tongue-tied among other people. Here also we have the individual attempting to buy off the imagined danger by propitiation*.

"At this level we have withdrawal from people."

1.1 Covert Hostility

"At 1.1, we have lying, to avoid real communication. It takes the form of pretended agreement, flattery or verbal appeasement* or simply a false picture of the person's feelings and ideas, an artificial personality. Here is the level of covert hostility, the most dangerous and wicked level on the Tone Scale. Here is the person who smiles while he inserts a knife blade in your vertebrae*. Here is the person who told you he stood up for you, when actually he has practically destroyed your reputation. Here is the insincere flatterer who yet awaits only a moment of unguardedness to destroy.

"The conversation of this level is filled with small barbs which are immediately afterwards justified as intended compliments. Talking with such a person is the maddening procedure of boxing with a shadow: one realizes that something is wrong, but the guardedness of a 1.1 will not admit anything wrong, even as, all the while he does his best to upset and wreak havoc.

"From such a person one should never expect a frontal attack; the attack will come when one is absent, when one's back is turned, or when one sleeps.

"A 1.1 can be accurately spotted by his conversation, since he seeks only to enturbulate* those around him, to upset them by his conversation, to destroy them without their ever being aware of his purpose.

"Here we have painstaking efforts to 'better people' by showing them their faults. Here we have attempts to "educate" people into adjusting them to their environment—in other words, to stop being vital and active and go somewhere and lie down, where they will be no menace.

"Above this level, but before we reach 1.5 (anger), the individual sinks into stubborn silence, sulks*, refuses to talk. He will not listen to any communication of any kind from other people, except that which encourages him in his attitude."

1.5 Anger

"In the lower band of anger, the person will look away from you, deliberately. It's an overt communication break.

"At this tone level, we have a shutting off of another person's conversation, a complete refusal to listen and efforts to destroy incoming conversation. The conversation which is given forth by an individual at this level is forthrightly destructive and is given without any thought of the possible retaliation which may result from this destructiveness. Conversation on this level could hardly be called conversation (the prefix con - meaning 'with' or 'together'), as it is a forward motion toward destruction and a refusal to accept anything which might prevent that destruction."

2.0 Antagonism

"At 2.0, antagonism, the person will look directly at you all right, but not very pleasantly. He wants to locate you—as a target.

"This is the level of antagonistic conversation. The individual is apt to nag or make derogatory comments to invalidate* other people. On this level the individual can only be roused by nagging, nasty cracks, invalidations and other antagonistic communication.

"At the level of tone 2.0, affinity is expressed as antagonism, a feeling of annoyance and irritation caused by the advances of other people toward the individual."

2.5 Boredom

"At boredom, you get the eyes wandering around again, but not frantically as in fear. Also, he won't be avoiding looking at you. He'll include you among the things he looks at.

"Here we have the level of indifference to conversation with others, a 'let's not argue about it' attitude, a dismissal of communication, a carelessness as to whether one's conversation is being received or is even understandable.

"Between 2.5 and 2.0 we have a level where communication from other people is refused, and where one does not like to talk.

"Boredom is not a state of inaction. It is a state of idle action."

3.0 Conservatism

"At 3.0, conservatism, the speech of the individual becomes casual and reserved. Here is the level of small talk, for example, about the weather. At this level the individual has a resistance toward ideas which are too massive (big or huge).

"Safety, security and somewhat better survival conditions are the arguments used along this level of the Tone Scale.

"At 3.0 on the scale, a person has a conservative, cautious aspect toward life but is reaching his goals."

3.5 Strong Interest

"At 3.5, strong interest, the individual is capable of communicating deeply-felt beliefs and ideas to others and can hold back or give forth conversation according to the rational or pleasant circumstances of the moment.

"The individual at this level can listen without becoming critical and can aid and assist others in conversation."

4.0 Enthusiasm

"At 4.0 the individual is enthusiastic, happy and vital.

"At this level, the individual experiences love, strong and outgoing; he experiences friendliness.

"At this high level, the individual is able to listen to everything which is said and evaluate it rationally. He can receive ideas without making critical or derogatory comments. And, while receiving another person's ideas, he can greatly aid that person's thinking and talking."

There are other tone levels in addition to the ones given here. The idea for now is to gain an understanding of the scale *as a scale* and to understand what each of the tones represents.

Social Tone versus Chronic Tone

Keep in mind there is a social tone level and there is a chronic tone level.

The social tone level is the tone that the person wants people around them to believe they are in. The chronic tone level is the tone they are actually in. The difference between these two tone levels can be significant.

A person may come across to you as very sweet and very social and very friendly. This indeed may be the case. Then again, it may be that this is the social tone level that is being presented to you and to others. What is beneath this social presentation? The person's actual and chronic tone level is beneath this. And it is VERY, VERY important for you to be able to differentiate between these two tone levels.

There are some exercises given in the next chapter that will help you differentiate between the social and chronic tones of a person.

HUBBARD CHART OF HUMAN EVALUATION*

Hubbard Chart of Human Evaluation

	1 Behavior and Physiology	2 Medical Range	3 Emotion	4 Sexual Behavior / Attitude Toward Children	5 Command Over Environment	6 Actual Worth to Society Compared to Apparent Worth	7 Ethic Level	8 Handling of Truth
Tone Scale 4.0	Excellent at projects, execution. Fast creation time (relative to age).	Near accident-proof. No psychosomatic ills. Nearly immune to bacteria.	Eagerness, exhilaration.	Sexual interest high but often sublimated to creative thought. Intense interest in children.	High self-mastery. Aggressive toward environ. Dislikes to control people. High reasoning, volatile emotions.	High worth. Apparent worth will be realized. Creative and constructive.	Bases ethics on reason. Very high ethic level.	High concept of truth.
3.5	Good at projects, execution, sports.	Highly resistant to common infections. No colds.	Strong interest.	High interest in opposite sex. Constancy. Love of children.	Reasons well. Good control. Accepts ownership. Emotion free. Liberal.	Good value to society. Adjusts environ to benefits of self and others.	Heeds ethics of group but refines them higher as reason demands.	Truthful.
3.0	Capable of fair amount of action, sports.	Resistant to infection and disease. Few psychosomatic ills.	Mild interest. Content.	Interest in procreation. Interest in children.	Controls bodily functions. Reasons well. Free emotion still inhibited. Allows rights to others. Democratic.	Any apparent worth is actual worth. Fair value.	Follows ethics in which trained as honestly as possible. Moral.	Cautious of asserting truths. Social lies.
2.5	Relatively inactive, but capable of action.	Occasionally ill. Susceptible to usual diseases.	Indifference. Boredom.	Disinterest in procreation. Vague tolerance of children.	In control of function and some reasoning powers. Does not desire much ownership.	Capable of constructive action, seldom much quantity. Small value. "Well adjusted."	Treats ethics insincerely. Not particularly honest or dishonest.	Insincere. Careless of facts.
2.0	Capable of destructive and minor constructive action.	Severe sporadic illnesses.	Expressed resentment.	Disgust at sex; revulsion. Nagging of and nervousness about children.	Antagonistic and destructive to self, others, and environ. Desires command in order to injure.	Dangerous. Any apparent worth wiped out by potentials of injury to others.	Below this point: authoritarian. Chronically and bluntly dishonest when occasion arises.	Truth twisted to suit antagonism.
1.5	Capable of destructive action.	Depository illnesses (arthritis). (Range 1.0 to 2.0 interchangeable.)	Anger.	Rape. Sex as punishment. Brutal treatment of children.	Smashes or destroys others or environ. Failing this, may destroy self. Fascistic.	Insincere. Heavy liability. Possible murderer. Even when intentions avowedly good will bring about destruction.	Below this point: criminal. Immoral. Actively dishonest. Destructive of any and all ethics.	Blatant and destructive lying.
1.1	Capable of minor execution.	Endocrine and neurological illnesses.	Unexpressed resentment. Fear.	Promiscuity, perversion, sadism, irregular practices. Use of children for sadistic purposes.	No control of reason or emotions, but apparent organic control. Uses sly means of controlling others, especially hypnotism. Communistic.	Active liability. Enturbulates[1] others. Apparent worth outweighed by vicious hidden intents.	Sex criminal. Negative ethics. Deviously dishonest without reason. Pseudoethical activities screen perversion of ethics.	Ingenious and vicious perversions of truth. Covers lying artfully.
0.5	Capable of relatively uncontrolled action.	Chronic malfunction of organs. (Accident-prone.)	Grief. Apathy.	Impotency, anxiety, possible efforts to reproduce. Anxiety about children.	Barely functional control of self only.	Liability to society. Possible suicide. Utterly careless of others.	Nonexistent. Not thinking. Obeying anyone.	Details facts with no concept of their reality.
0.1	Alive as an organism.	Chronically ill. (Refusing sustenance.)	Deepest apathy.	No effort to procreate.	No command of self, others, environ. Suicide.	High liability, needing care and efforts of others without making any contribution.	None	No reaction.

1. **enturbulate:** cause to be turbulent or agitated and disturbed.

9 COURAGE LEVEL	10 SPEECH: TALKS / SPEECH: LISTENS	11 SUBJECT'S HANDLING OF WRITTEN OR SPOKEN COMM[3] WHEN ACTING AS A RELAY POINT	12 REALITY (AGREEMENT)	13 ABILITY TO HANDLE RESPONSIBILITY	14 PERSISTENCE ON A GIVEN COURSE	15 LITERALNESS OF RECEPTION OF STATEMENTS	16 METHOD USED BY SUBJECT TO HANDLE OTHERS	Tone Scale
High courage level.	Strong, able, swift and full exchange of beliefs and ideas.	Passes theta comm, contributes to it. Cuts entheta[4] lines.	Search for different viewpoints in order to broaden own reality. Changes reality.	Inherent sense of responsibility in all areas of life.	High creative persistence.	High differentiation. Good understanding of all communication.	Gains support by creative enthusiasm and vitality backed by reason.	4.0
Courage displayed on reasonable risks.	Will talk of deep-seated beliefs and ideas. / Will accept deep-seated beliefs, ideas; consider them.	Passes theta comm. Resents and hits back at entheta lines.	Ability to understand and evaluate reality of others and to change viewpoint. Agreeable.	Capable of assuming and carrying on responsibilities.	Good persistence and direction toward constructive goals.	Good grasp of statements. Good sense of humor.	Gains support by creative reasoning and vitality.	3.5
Conservative display of courage where risk is small.	Tentative expression of limited number of personal ideas. / Receives ideas and beliefs, if cautiously stated.	Passes comm. Conservative. Inclines toward moderate construction and creation.	Awareness of possible validity of different reality. Conservative agreement.	Handles responsibility in a slipshod fashion.	Fair persistence if obstacles not too great.	Good differentiation of meaning of statements.	Invites support by practical reasoning and social graces.	3.0
Neither courage nor cowardice. Neglect of danger.	Casual pointless conversation. / Listens only to ordinary affairs.	Cancels any comm of higher or lower tone. Devaluates urgencies.	Refusal to match two realities. Indifference to conflict in reality. Too careless to agree or disagree.	Too careless. Not trustworthy.	Idle, poor concentration.	Accepts very little, literally or otherwise. Apt to be literal about humor.	Careless of support from others.	2.5
Reactive, unreasoning thrusts at danger.	Talks in threats. Invalidates other people. / Listens to threats. Openly mocks theta[2] talk.	Deals in hostile or threatening comm. Lets only small amount of theta go through.	Verbal doubt. Defense of own reality. Attempts to undermine others. Disagrees.	Uses responsibility to further own ends.	Persistence toward destruction of enemies. No constructive persistence below this point.	Accepts remarks of tone 2.0 literally.	Nags and bluntly criticizes to demand compliance with wishes.	2.0
Unreasonable bravery, usually damaging to self.	Talks of death, destruction, hate only. / Listens only to death and destruction. Wrecks theta lines.	Perverts comm to entheta regardless of original content. Stops theta comm. Passes entheta and perverts it.	Destruction of opposing reality: "You're wrong." Disagrees with reality of others.	Assumes responsibility in order to destroy.	Destructive persistence begins strongly, weakens quickly.	Accepts alarming remarks literally. Brutal sense of humor.	Uses threats, punishment and alarming lies to dominate others.	1.5
Occasional underhanded displays of action, otherwise cowardly.	Talks apparent theta, but intent vicious. / Listens little, mostly to cabal, gossip, lies.	Relays only malicious comm. Cuts comm lines. Won't relay.	Doubt of own reality. Insecurity. Doubt of opposing reality.	Incapable, capricious irresponsible.	Vacillation on any course. Very poor concentration. Flighty.	Lack of acceptance of any remarks. Tendency to accept all literally avoided by forced humor.	Nullifies others to get them to level where they can be used. Devious and vicious means. Hypnotism, gossip. Seeks hidden control.	1.1
Complete cowardice.	Talks very little and only in apathetic tones. / Listens little: mostly to apathy or pity.	Takes little heed of comm. Does not relay.	Shame, anxiety, strong doubt of own reality. Easily has reality of others forced on him.	None.	Sporadic persistence toward self-destruction.	Literal acceptance of any remark matching tone.	Enturbulates others to control them. Cries for pity. Wild lying to gain sympathy.	0.5
No reaction.	Does not talk. / Does not listen.	Does not relay. Unaware of comm.	Complete withdrawal from conflicting reality. No reality.	None.	None.	Complete literal acceptance.	Pretends death so others will not think him dangerous and will go away.	0.1

2. **theta:** reason, serenity, stability, happiness, cheerful emotion, persistence, and the other factors which man ordinarily considers desirable.
3. **comm:** communication.
4. **entheta:** especially refers to communications, which, based on lies and confusion, are slanderous, choppy or destructive.

Hubbard Chart of Human Evaluation

17 Hypnotic Level **18** Ability to Experience Present Time Pleasure **19** Your Value as a Friend **20** How Much Others Like You **21** State of Your Possessions **22** How Well Are You Understood **23** Potential Success **24** Potential Survival

17	18	19	20	21	22	23	24	
Impossible to hypnotize without drugs.	Finds existence very full of pleasure.	Excellent.	Loved by many.	In excellent condition.	Very well.	Excellent.	Excellent. Considerable longevity.	Tone Scale 4.0
Difficult to trance.	Finds life pleasurable most of the time.	Very good.	Well loved.	In good condition.	Well.	Very good.	Very good.	3.5
Could be hypnotized but alert when awake.	Experiences pleasure some of the time.	Good.	Respected by most.	Fairly good.	Usually.	Good.	Good.	3.0
Can be a hypnotic subject, but mostly alert.	Experiences moments of pleasure. Low intensity.	Fair.	Liked by a few.	Shows some neglect.	Sometimes misunderstood.	Fair.	Fair.	2.5
Negates somewhat, but can be hypnotized.	Occasionally experiences some pleasure in extraordinary moments.	Poor.	Rarely liked.	Very neglected.	Often misunderstood.	Poor.	Poor.	2.0
Negates heavily against remarks, but absorbs them.	Seldom experiences any pleasure.	Definite liability.	Openly disliked by most.	Often broken. Bad repair.	Continually misunderstood.	Usually a failure.	Early demise.	1.5
In a permanent light trance, but negates.	Most gaiety forced. Real pleasure out of reach.	Dangerous liability.	Generally despised.	Poor. In poor condition.	No real understanding.	Nearly always fails.	Brief.	1.1
Very hypnotic. Any remark made may be a "positive suggestion."	None.	Very great liability.	Not liked. Only pitied by some.	In very bad condition generally.	Not at all understood.	Utter failure.	Demise soon.	0.5
Is equivalent to a hypnotized subject when "awake."	None.	Total liability.	Not regarded.	No realization of possession.	Ignored.	No effort. Complete failure.	Almost dead.	0.1

Chapter Thirteen

THE CHART OF HUMAN EVALUATION

One of the best ways to utilize The Emotional Tone Scale is in conjunction with the Hubbard Chart of Human Evaluation.

From the works of L. Ron Hubbard, we learn the following:

> *"The whole subject of how to accurately judge our fellows is something man has wanted to be able to do for a long time. We now have a chart which shows a way one can precisely evaluate* human behavior and predict what a person will do.*
>
> *"This is the Hubbard Chart of Human Evaluation. The chart displays the degree of ethics*, responsibility, persistence on a given course, handling of truth and other identifying aspects of a person along the various levels of the Tone Scale.*
>
> *"You can examine the chart and you will find in the boxes, as you go across it, the various characteristics of people at these levels. Horribly enough these characteristics have been found to be constant. If you have a 3.0 as your rating, then you will carry across the whole chart at 3.0*
>
> *"If you can locate two or three characteristics along a certain level of this scale, you can look in the number column opposite those characteristics and find the level. It may be 2.5, it may be 1.5. Wherever it is, simply look at all the columns opposite the number you found and you will see the remaining characteristics.*
>
> *"The only mistake you can make in evaluating somebody else on this Tone Scale is to assume that he departs from it somewhere and is higher in one department than he is in another. The characteristic may be masked to which you object—but it is there.*
>
> *"Look at the top of the first column and you get a general picture of the behavior and physiology* of the person. Look at the second column for the*

physical condition. Look at the third column for the most generally expressed emotion of the person. Continue on across the various columns. Somewhere you will find data about somebody or yourself of which you can be sure. Then simply examine all the other boxes at the level of the data you were certain about. That band, be it 1.5 or 3.0 will tell you the story of a human being.

"Of course, as good news and bad, happy days and sad ones, strike a person, there are momentary raises and lowerings on this Tone Scale. But, as mentioned, there is a chronic level, an average behavior for each individual.

"As an individual is found lower and lower on this chart, so is his alertness, his consciousness lower and lower.

... "One's environment also greatly influences one's position on the chart. Every environment has its own tone level. A man who is really 3.0 can begin to act like a 1.1 (covert hostility) in a 1.1 environment. However, a 1.1 usually acts no better than about 1.5 in an environment with a high tone. If one lives in a low-toned environment he can expect, eventually, to be low-toned. This is also true of a marriage—one tends to match the tone level of one's marital partner.

"This Tone Scale is also valid for groups. A business or a nation can be examined as to its various standard reactions and these can be plotted. This will give the survival potential of a business or a nation.

"This chart can also be used in employing people or in choosing partners. It is an accurate index of what to expect and gives you a chance to predict what people will do before you have any great experience with them. Also, it gives you some clue as to what can happen to you in certain environments or around certain people, for they can drag you down or boost you high.

"However don't use this chart as an effort to make somebody knuckle under*. Don't tell people where they are on it. It may ruin them. Let them make their own examinations.

"A Tone Scale Test

"Probably the most accurate index of a person's position on the Tone Scale is speech.

"*Unless a person talks openly and listens receptively he cannot be considered very high on the Tone Scale.*

"*In column 10 of the Hubbard Chart of Human Evaluation, 'Speech: Talks/Speech: Listens', there are double boxes: one set referring to talking, the other to listening. It may not have occurred to some people that communication is both outflow and inflow. An observation of how a person both listens and talks will give an accurate indication of his position on the Tone Scale.*

"*It is interesting to note that with this column one can conduct what we call a 'two-minute psychometry' on someone.* Psychometry *is the measurement of mental traits, abilities and processes. The way to do a two-minute psychometry is simply to start talking to the person at the highest possible tone level, creatively and constructively, and then gradually drop the tone of one's conversation down to the point where it achieves response from the person.*

"*An individual best responds to his own tone band; and an individual can be lifted only about a half a point on the Tone Scale by conversation. In doing this type of 'psychometry', one should not carry any particular band of conversation too long, not more than a sentence or two, because this will have a tendency to raise slightly the tone of the person and so spoil the accuracy of the test.*

"*Two-minute psychometry, then, is done, first, by announcing something creative and constructive and seeing whether the person responds in kind; then, giving forth some casual conversation, perhaps about sports, and seeing if the person responds to that.*

"*Getting no response start talking antagonistically about things about which the person knows—but not, of course, about the person—to see if he achieves a response at this point.*

"*Then give forth with a sentence or two of anger against some condition.*

"*Then indulge in a small amount of discreditable* gossip and see if there is any response to that.*

"*If this does not work, then dredge up some statements of hopelessness and misery. Somewhere in this range the person will agree with the type of conversation that is being offered — that is, he will respond to it in kind. A conversation can then be carried on along this band where the person has*

> been discovered, and one will rapidly gain enough information to make a good first estimate of the person's position on the chart.
>
> "This two-minute psychometry by conversation can also be applied to groups. That speaker who desires to command his audience must not talk above or below his audience's tone more than half a point. If he wishes to lift the audience's tone, he should talk about half a point above their general tone level. An expert speaker, using this two-minute psychometry and carefully noting the responses of his audience, can, in two minutes, discover the tone of the audience — whereupon, all he has to do is adopt a tone slightly above theirs.
>
> "The Tone Scale and the Chart of Human Evaluation are the most important tools ever developed for the prediction of human behavior. Employ these tools and you will at all times know who you are dealing with, who to associate with, who to trust."

There are many ways you can use the data of the Tone Scale and The Chart of Human Evaluation to assist you in your relationships.

If you are unsure about starting a meaningful relationship with someone, do the two minute psychometry test on them and determine their tone level. Then, on the Chart of Human Evaluation, look down the entire row of that tone level and you will see what kind of person you are considering. Your decision will be made an awful lot easier.

What about marrying someone? If you know the person's tone level, look him (or her) up on the Chart of Human Evaluation. It will not lie to you. If you are not sure what the person's tone level is, then either use the two minute psychometry test or go down various columns of the Chart of Human Evaluation and locate two or three characteristics about this person on which you are certain. Then look for the number that represents that tone level. Now you have a complete picture of your prospective mate — all of the characteristics of that level are a part of that person.

I remind you of a point that Mr. Hubbard made about this Tone Scale:

> "The only mistake you can make in evaluating somebody else on this Tone Scale is to assume that he departs from it somewhere and is higher in one department than he is in another. The characteristic may be masked to which you object—but it is there."

CHAPTER 13 — *The Chart Of Human Evaluation*

Here are two exercises that will help you use these tools:

EXERCISES

1) Go up to 3 people you have never met and do the two-minute psychometry test with them. Determine each person's tone level. Now do this with more people until you can comfortably do this with anyone.

2) Locate on the Chart of Human Evaluation someone you know. Go down the various columns until you find characteristics about this person that you are sure about and then locate the person's tone that corresponds with these characteristics. Do this with other people you know until you are certain you can use the chart in this way.

The above two exercises are worth their weight in gold. Get yourself very familiar with The Tone Scale. Get yourself fully acquainted with the Chart of Human Evaluation.

When you know the tone level of someone, you will then be able to predict what kinds of things that person will do, and what kinds of things will happen in the environment of that person. The Chart of Human Evaluation will tell you in incredible detail what you can expect. It is almost impossible to place a value on this kind of knowledge.

The Emotional Tone Scale can be used in a variety of ways. Let's go into some detail on this. L. Ron Hubbard says the following:

> *"Is there some kind of a system by which you ... can get some agreement and cooperation from a person in apathy? In grief? In fear? In antagonism? In boredom? In conservatism? Is there some kind of method by which you can get good agreement so that these people will go along with you? Yes, and it is about as simple as it comes. You just match the person's tone.*
>
> *"Let's apply this to an angry man. You want to sell something to this fellow in anger and you say to him, 'It's a beautiful day, isn't it?' That isn't going to work! Instead, you better take a look at him, listen to his voice tones and look at his office help.*
>
> *"For example, let's say you are working on the financing of a project to build a city park. You walk into the office of this angry fellow just as he is saying, 'They all ought to be stood up against a wall ...'*
>
> *"You say, 'And shot!'*
>
> *"He looks at you and says with relief, 'Soul mate!'*

" 'Now,' you ask, 'who should be stood up against a wall?'

" 'Those dogs, that's who!'

" 'Well, it's just like this project! If we had this project, we could shoot 'em!'

" 'What project?' he asks, interested.

"The project we are using in this example is to build a city park. To someone in anger, you don't want the park for the kids and someplace to let the birds sing. The reason you want to build this city park is to get even with those contractors that wanted the land. Something like that will sell this angry fellow on a city park. He will write out his check.

"It is a sympathetic vibration*.

"Did you ever see the physics class experiment where you have two tuning forks[2] side by side? If you hit only one of them, the other one will vibrate too, even if you damp* out the first one.

"That is a sympathetic vibration. You have to talk along a sympathy* line. I don't mean the sympathy of grief. You have to match the tone level that this person normally frequents.

"You could be fooled. You cold look at this fellow and say to yourself that he looks like a conservative old man and start talking to him more or less conservatively. 'We have this large conservative project and it's going to do a lot of good and it's going to make some money.' You don't talk about this project making anybody happy, but you tell him, 'It does good and it's practical and it's going to make some money.' You talk to him like that, and the first thing you know, this fellow says apathetically, 'Well, I don't think anybody would live to use it in these times.' You were wrong.

"To sell to someone in apathy, you would say, 'Of course, it probably won't do any good anyway.'

"If you were trying to sell him a tractor, you would say, 'Most of them around the countryside are all broken; they don't last very long. Almost any competitor of ours is outselling us anyhow. They don't work.' He will sigh, 'Well, give me one.'

"All too often an individual who is trying to do business with other individuals, who is trying to work with other individuals, will be so solidly fixed in a tone himself that he doesn't understand the necessity of trying to get *into communication with another individual* before *he tries to do something* with *him. It is necessary to get into communication first. The only way you can get into good, solid communication anywhere along this line is to match the person on the Tone Scale.*

"An insurance salesman who is fixed at the line of fear goes around and tells everybody to be afraid. He tells them in various ways. He goes on selling, 'Be afraid, be afraid, be afraid, be afraid.' He is an excellent salesman if the community in which he is selling has a predominance of people at this tone level. But he would completely flop if he were trying to sell this idea to higher-toned people. Suppose he tried to sell it in the offices of a very conservative magazine. He would go in and say, 'Be afraid, be afraid,' and they would put a cartoon in the magazine about somebody being afraid. They would not be impressed and they would not react. This individual who is fixed at the level of fear can only get a reaction at the level of fear.

"Educationally, this person could begin to understand that not everybody was at his tone level, that maybe there was somebody at apathy. You give the person in apathy this pitch, 'Be afraid, be afraid, be afraid, be afraid'—standard insurance arguments. This person would *like* to be afraid. Fear is two rungs up the Tone Scale! He isn't afraid. The only way you could sell him anything at all would be to tell him, 'This is a recognition of the fact that there is no fear involved anyplace in the world anyhow, and there's no use in doing this stuff and it doesn't have any end or purpose. But people would sure think you were dead. It really proves the fact that a man is practically on his way out to have a policy of this size, doesn't it?'

" 'Yes, it does. Where's my fountain pen?'

"You can't sell it to him on the basis of 'You know, you ought to have this because you're going to die and your wife is liable to be left penniless.'

"Wife? The person in apathy has had no emotional response about anybody but himself for so long, you can't sell him anything about any other part of his environment. You can't even sell him well on himself. He is way down there.

"The person in grief is sitting there saying, 'It's all hopeless. There is no future. I wouldn't bring a child into this world anyway. Things are pretty horrible over there in Europe anyway. I know when my husband used to beat me, I used to say...' "

"And you just say, 'You poor thing. We feel sorry for you. I feel sorry for you. Everybody feels sorry for you. Sign on the dotted line. Everybody feels sorry for you.' That's all a person in grief can hear.

... "You are trying to match grief. Grief doesn't listen. It is senseless, when a person breaks down and starts to cry, for you to say, 'It's all right. Life is going to be beautiful, life is going to be wonderful. The sun will shine again.' ... You can stand there and talk like that for a long time but about the only thing you can do is to pat them on the shoulder and say, 'I feel sorry for you. Yes, everybody feels sorry for you. We pity you.' And if you carry along in that line this person will finally simmer down and smooth out very nicely. You can get a communication line then because grief is a supplication* and plea for pity.

"But on a fear level, you can only sell things that prevent death. Here is where the political parties really come in. Imagine a populace which is predominantly in a state of fear. I don't mean that they are specifically afraid of something. They are just in a fixed state of fear. They have been up against politicians a long time and they are scared stiff.

"Somebody talking along the line of 'Be happy and cheer up because all is well tomorrow' is not going to win the election. The fellow who is going to win the election from this populace is the fellow who says, 'We are being attacked from all sides by enemies! The subversives* are coming in underneath and prying us apart. ...The country must be saved! This is a time for emergency measures! I'll save you from all this! We need price controls and...'

"Fear is best appealed to by arguments about things to be afraid of. Anger is best appealed to by things to be angry about.

"Something else happens when you skip a tone. Boredom can more or less dampen out antagonism. Anger can control fear. Fear can play on down to grief a little bit. If we are speaking in terms of two people, side by side, the one who will more or less be in command of the other will be the one who is a grade up from the other one.

"Conservative people, uniformly throughout the society, depend almost exclusively upon the dreamer and the happy individual to provide the ideas which provide conservatism with its action. You have noticed that. Actually, to the conservative there is a necessity to put something together well. However, there is no reason why practicality can't be happy.

> *"A populace which is at 2.5, which is just bored, can be ruled by a conservative government—a reasonable, practical, conservative government. However, a society which is at 1.1 cannot be ruled by a conservative, practical government; it can only be ruled by an angry or antagonistic government.*
>
> *"Agreement occurs at the same emotional tone level as the person making the statement. He buys his facts at that level.*
>
> *"To go half a tone to a tone up from a person's level is to command him within his zone of reality.*
>
> *"…To control a Tone Scale point you move half a tone to a tone above it.*
>
> *"Doing this with a person you can bring him up tone and impress him. People will go into* agreement, *at their own tone, but they are not* impressed *with their own tone."*

Let's go over this some more and see how this can help you in your relationships.

First of all, Mr. Hubbard talks about the importance of matching* a person's tone level if you want to gain agreement from that person. Have you experienced trying to get somebody to do something and no matter how much you reason with the person, or how much you urge the person, you just don't seem to get real agreement with this person? You were probably approaching this person in the wrong tone level! Yes, it could be that simple!

Let's say you have an employee who is in the tone level of, say, "boredom", and you try to excite and enthuse him to get going, get productive, get moving…and you just don't make any headway. What's happening here? You are simply too high on the tone scale to make any real impact on this person. If you then went back to this employee and communicated to him from this tone level of "boredom" and talked about things to be bored about, you would find yourself in communication with him. Getting people to do things depends initially on being in communication with them!

And Mr. Hubbard says the easiest and most effective way to get in communication with someone is to match their tone.

How about somebody who is in the tone level of "enthusiasm"? How would this person respond to somebody who was always being antagonistic? Not very well at all!

Do you think somebody who was genuinely an enthusiastic person would believe things said by a person constantly in fear of things? Not hardly.

It has to do with their tone level. Their tone level is the emotional state that they most normally frequent. It exists somewhere on the Tone Scale. If you know what somebody's tone level is, you can gain their agreement by matching their tone.

Then, if you want to make some real headway, after you've matched their tone level and gained their agreement, you move a half a notch* to a full notch above that tone and you will find you can accomplish all kinds of things with this person.

Another example: let's say you are doing a presentation to someone who is somewhat antagonistic. This person shows the various characteristics of the tone level of "antagonism". (If necessary, turn back to the page that explains "antagonism" in detail). In this example, you're a doctor and you are trying to get this person to purchase a treatment plan that you know they need.

The person is making various critical comments about how all doctors are just filthy rich and make all kinds of money doing things that people really don't need done to them. After listening to this for a little while, you look the patient straight in the face and say: "I agree! Those doctors should all be packed up and taken to an island somewhere where they can all work on each other!"

The patient sits back in his chair and expresses a sigh of relief, thinking "now, here's somebody that understands me!"

You have now matched his tone level and gained some agreement from him. You may want to continue along this line for a little while longer to ensure you have fully matched his tone level, but your object is to get a half to a full notch above this level of antagonism, so what do we do now?

Well, antagonism is at 2.0. A full notch up is "conservatism" at 3.0. Let's try this:

After you've matched his tone level at "antagonism," you move up to conservatism and say: "Well, I certainly can see what you're saying. I like to take a practical approach to one's physical health. After this treatment program, your body will be stronger and healthier. I like dealing with things in a safe and practical manner."

This will not only diffuse the person's antagonism, this tone of "conservatism" (at 3.0), which is one full notch above antagonism (at 2.0), will actually help to guide the communication cycle to its intended end — the person agreeing to experience the benefits of the treatment plan.

Remember, Mr. Hubbard said:

> *"Agreement occurs at the same emotional tone level as the person making the statement. He buys his facts at that level.*
>
> *"To go half a tone to a tone up from a person's level is to command him within his zone of reality."*

You establish agreement with the person by matching his tone level. You have his agreement, and he will buy his facts at that level. To then command him within his zone of reality means that you need to move one half to a full notch above that tone level.

Let's look at another example. Let's say you have an employee who seems always to be in grief. She may not always be crying, but she seems to be a griefy-type person. She is in the tone level of grief. This tone level is very low on the Emotional Tone Scale and you may want to keep a close eye on this person's performance, but in the meantime, let's figure out how we can get this person contributing more to the business.

It may take a little effort on your part, but you should approach someone in the tone level of grief from the point of view of: "you poor thing. Everyone pities you. Oh, you poor thing." A person truly in grief will genuinely respond to this kind of communication.

We observe that the tone level of "fear" is half a notch above "grief". Okay, then we start talking to this person about things that someone might be afraid of: "Well, Mary, I certainly understand your difficulties. I'm afraid of what may happen around here if we don't get this project finished that you're working on. It makes me fearful just to think about it."

"Fear" is half a notch above "grief." And if Mary is chronically in this tone level of "grief", then this kind of communication delivered at that tone level will be effective.

If you feel that using the Tone Scale in communicating to others is a form of manipulation, then consider this: folks who are low on the Tone Scale have been using their low tone to manipulate others for a long, long time. Covertly hostile people use the tone of covert hostility to accomplish things that may not be in the best interest of others. People in the tone of "apathy" spend a good deal of their lives trying to bring others closer to their tone. If you recall different encounters with people low on the Tone Scale (below 2.0) you may recall that you came out of those encounters feeling less alive, less certain, less outgoing.

As mentioned earlier, there are two different types of tone levels. There is the social tone level. This is the one that the person presents to you and to the world around them. This is the tone level that they want you to think they are in. Often a person will present a much higher tone than they actually are. Their real tone level is their chronic tone level. This is the one that really governs their behavior. It is sometimes very hidden, but it is there.

The two minute psychometry test, mentioned earlier, is a tool that can help you locate the chronic tone level. You can also locate someone's chronic position on the Tone Scale by use of the Hubbard Chart of Human Evaluation. However you do it, realize the chronic tone and the social tone are not necessarily the same tone level. When you are interested in a person's tone, you are interested in their chronic tone. Their social tone is the tone that they want you to believe they are in, but the chronic tone gives you the true picture.

All of us are familiar with the person who comes up to you and compliments you in some way, but you go away not feeling complimented at all. This is the 1.1. The covertly hostile person. They are not openly hostile, they haven't the courage to be openly hostile. So they manage to express their hostility in covert ways. This is the person who smiles right to your face, while conceiving of some way to undermine or make less of you.

Example: a covertly hostile person (1.1 on the Tone Scale) comes into your office and says: "Well, boss, I guess you've done the best you can with Bill. He really wasn't cut out to be a salesperson, but you've sure done what you can with him." Somehow you really don't feel very complimented by this communication. You've been told how Bill really isn't much of anything and that you've done what you can with him… it's an attempt at a compliment, but it is hostility expressed covertly.

How would you handle this kind of person? Well, you can certainly match their tone quickly to gain their agreement. But you may want to quickly move a half to a full notch above this 1.1 level. Let's choose "antagonism". That's 2.0 on the scale and that will certainly fit the bill.

After our 1.1 has dropped his covertly hostile compliment on the table for you, you look him straight in the eye and say: "Do me a favor. Spare me the left handed compliments! I don't need to be reminded of other people's inadequacies. I'm trying to build a team here. Please start acting like a team member!"

Your response to this covertly hostile person will tell him that his covert comments are not welcome and he will be much less likely to continue in that vein. You are using the tone of "antagonism" to control the tone below it of "covert hostility". It will work and it will work splendidly.

Keep a VERY close eye on a truly 1.1 person. Observe very impartially the effects this person has on others around them.

Using the Tone Scale to Improve Relationships

You have seen from the above examples that you can significantly improve the level of communication with someone if you match the person's tone level.

The more you understand this Tone Scale, and the more you use it in your everyday relationships, the smoother your relationships will move along. People respond extremely well when you communicate to them at their tone level. When you then move a half of a notch to a full notch above that tone, you will find even more positive things happening. Where there was less affinity, there will now be more affinity.

At the end of this chapter, there are drills for you to do to become more comfortable with matching someone's tone level. These drills will also make it easier for you to go a half to a full notch above the person's tone level.

How do you keep YOURSELF high-toned? Mr. Hubbard created very specific procedures that will not only keep a person high-toned, but can also bring a lower-toned person into a higher tone level.

For immediate purposes, one way to keep yourself high-toned is to surround yourself with high-toned people. You could be very ruthless about this and just not allow low-toned people in your life. However, the world has a fairly large segment of low-toned folks in it, so this is not always a realistic course of action.

Knowing where people fall on this Tone Scale and knowing how they will respond to various situations in life will put you more and more in command of your own life. Using this information will help every single one of your relationships.

EXERCISES

1) Go up to 3 people and determine their tone level. (Use the technique described earlier in the chapter: Two Minute Psychometry). Then try to talk to them several levels above or below their tone level and observe the results of this. Then match their tone level and see what happens. Do this with more people until you are comfortable matching someone's tone AND you are certain of its effects.

2) Go up to 3 different people and first match their tone level. Then go a half to one full notch above their tone and communicate to them from this tone. Note how they respond when you move (a half to a full notch) **above** their tone and how they responded **at** their tone. Do this with more people until you are comfortable doing this AND you are certain of its effects.

The Emotional Tone Scale and the Hubbard Chart of Evaluation will help you with every one of your relationships.

Here is an excellent investment you can make towards your future success: spend some time every week doing the above drills; get yourself expert at spotting tone levels and understanding the Tone Scale and the Chart of Human Evaluation. Use each of these tools as fully as you can!

The book *Science of Survival* by L. Ron Hubbard goes over The Chart of Human Evaluation in even greater detail. Mr. Hubbard also gave a series of lectures entitled *The Special Course in Human Evaluation*. This lecture series covers the theory behind the Tone Scale and gives numerous ways it can be effectively used.

To obtain a copy of *Science of Survival*, or *The Special Course in Human Evaluation*, see the order form at the end of this book.

Chapter Fourteen

KNOWLEDGE RESPONSIBILITY AND CONTROL

This chapter gives you another tool to help your relationships succeed. In Chapter 8, the "ARC Triangle" was presented. The ARC Triangle is composed of affinity, reality and communication. If you raise any corner of this ARC triangle, the other two corners also increase. The same is true of this next triangle. It is called the "KRC Triangle".

The three corners of this triangle are:

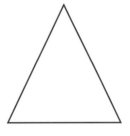

L. Ron Hubbard says the following about this extremely useful triangle:

"There is a triangle that ... applies to anyone. It has not been widely known.

"It is the K—R—C triangle. The points are K for KNOWLEDGE*, R for RESPONSIBILITY* and C for CONTROL*.

"It is difficult to be responsible for something or control something unless you have KNOWLEDGE of it.

"It is folly to try to control something or even know something without RESPONSIBILITY.

"It is hard to fully know something or be responsible for something over which you have no CONTROL, otherwise the result can be an overwhelm.

> "A person can of course run away from life and go sit on the backside of the moon and do nothing and think nothing. In which case he would need to know nothing, be responsible for nothing and control nothing. He would also be unhappy and he definitely would be dead so far as himself and all else was concerned.
>
> "The route up from apathy or inaction is to KNOW something about it, take some RESPONSIBILITY for the state one is in and the scene, and CONTROL oneself to a point where some control is put into the scene to make it go right. Then KNOW why it went wrong, take RESPONSIBILITY for it, and CONTROL it enough to make it go more toward an ideal scene.
>
> "Little by little one can make anything go right by
>
> "INCREASING KNOWLEDGE in all areas of life.
>
> "INCREASING RESPONSIBILITY in all areas of life.
>
> "INCREASING CONTROL in all areas of life.
>
> "If one sorts out any situation one finds oneself in on this basis, he will generally succeed."

Mr. Hubbard goes on to say that these three areas of life: KNOWLEDGE, RESPONSIBILITY and CONTROL can be viewed in terms of a triangle. Similar to the ARC Triangle, you will notice that if you increase one corner of the triangle, the other two corners will go up. If you increase your knowledge of something, you will increase your ability to be responsible for it and you will increase your ability to control it.

If you have a situation in your relationship, and you don't feel you can confront it, you're certainly going to have a difficult time controlling it. Let's see how this triangle can help you with this situation.

One thing you can do is find out more about the situation. Increase your knowledge of it. However you choose to do this, simply increase your knowledge of it. Maybe you just go and ask a few questions about the situation. Maybe you read a few things about it. You're not trying to control the situation right now, you're just trying to increase your knowledge of it.

By applying this one corner of the triangle and by increasing your knowledge of the situation, you will find you have increased your ability to control and to be more responsible for the situation.

By the way, the opposite is also true. If you decide to take less RESPONSIBILITY for some area, you will instantly find that you are less able to CONTROL it and interestingly enough, you will find that you even KNOW less about it. The same is true of all three corners of the triangle. Increase or decrease one corner and the other corners will increase or decrease thereby.

Use of this triangle can dramatically improve your relationships.

It can be applied to other areas of your life: your business, your finances ... any nook and cranny* of your life will respond to this technology.

Additionally, Mr. Hubbard said:

> *"Most people have a dreadfully bad opinion of their capabilities compared to what they actually are. Hardly anybody believes himself capable of what he is really capable of accomplishing.*
>
> *"By inching up each corner of the KRC triangle bit by bit, ignoring the losses and making the wins firm, a person at length discovers his power and command of life."*

I suggest you take that last paragraph and type it out on a piece of paper and display it very visibly somewhere in your home (or office). If you inch up each corner of this triangle in any situation you find yourself in, AND if you ignore the losses and make the wins firm, you will at length discover your power and command of life.

Doing the Opposite Gets Us Nowhere

Do you know what too many people do? They ignore the wins and make the losses firm! In other words, if they have a loss, they dwell on it, perhaps talk an awful lot about it or go into blaming themselves or others for it. Have you ever found yourself spending all kinds of time thinking about a loss? I know I have! Somehow, all of that time didn't produce anything positive for me.

Well, you now have a completely different route to take in terms of losses you've had or may have: IGNORE THEM. Make a causative decision to ignore them. This may take a little practice, but don't underestimate the value of ignoring the losses.

And the other side of this coin is making the wins firm. This is a very important part of making this all work for you. When you have a win or achieve something good, take some time and effort and make it firm.

Let's say you or your spouse experience a boost in your income. Maybe one of you gets a raise. You could pat yourself on the back and get on with it. That's one approach. Another approach is to really acknowledge what happens.. Go out for a wonderful dinner. Really let the person know who got the raise that he/she did great.

What if the two of you had a particularly satisfying love making. Take a few minutes and really acknowledge each other for having accomplished that.

Make the Wins Firm!

There are countless ways to make the wins firm, but trust me—if you take some time when there's a gain or an accomplishment, and if you do something to make that gain or win firm, you will have more and more of them.

Do not treat this piece of technology lightly. This is very, very powerful stuff. As I said, many people ignore the wins and make the losses firm. And guess what? They have less and less wins and more and more losses. Take a few seconds and digest this concept: many people ignore the wins and make the losses firm ... reverse this approach— ignore the losses and make the wins firm.

Can it really be that simple? You'll never know unless you try. You may have to apply this tech for a little while to get it really going for you. Let's look at this quote one more time:

> *"By inching up each corner of the KRC triangle bit by bit, ignoring the losses and making the wins firm, a person at length discovers his power and command of life."*

You now have another tool to improve the quality of your relationships. Use it well. Let others in on it!

Chapter Fifteen

INCREASING YOUR ABILITY TO CONFRONT

The word "confront" has taken on some interesting connotations. If I were to say to you: "You need to confront Susan!", you would probably get the idea that there needed to be a confrontation, and that there could be some sparks.

This connotation of confronting is not the one we are interested in right now. We are interested in a much more basic definition.

Defined by L. Ron Hubbard, "to confront" is:

> *"to face without flinching or avoiding."*

This definition does not include the concept of some kind of an emotional confrontation. It is simply "to face without flinching or avoiding."

There are some things in life that we avoid facing. What we do in these cases is to simply look away or look at something else. In other words, instead of just simply confronting or facing something, we direct our attention to something else.

Some things in life cause us to flinch. We find these areas difficult to confront.

Your relationships may have various areas that you would rather avoid. If you do, those areas will cause problems for you. At some point along the line, any area of your relationship that you have difficulty facing or confronting, that area will cause problems for you.

Mr. Hubbard goes on to say:

> *"That which a person can confront, he can handle.*
>
> *"The first step of handling anything is gaining an ability to face it.*
>
> ... *"Problems start with an inability to confront anything.*

> .... *"The handling of a problem seems to be simply the increase of ability to confront the problem, and when the problem can be totally confronted, it no longer exists. This is strange and miraculous."*

I have applied this last paragraph to various situations of my life, and I have to admit the results were indeed strange and miraculous. In other words, when I totally confronted the problem, it no longer existed.

How can we apply this specifically to your relationships?

Well, the first step to handling anything is gaining an ability to face it.

What part of your relationship do you feel backed off from? What area of your relationship would you rather not face or confront?

Let's do this simple, but powerful exercise:

EXERCISE

1) Write down a list of problems you are having with your relationship.

2) Which of these problems is it easiest for you to confront? Write this problem down on a separate piece of paper.

3) Now decide what you are absolutely certain you can do about that problem. Write that down underneath this problem. Do NOT concern yourself if what you wrote down seemed very small in its potential effect —doing this entire exercise will work beautifully for you.

4) Now go off and DO this thing that you are absolutely certain you can do.

5) What other part of this problem are you now certain you can do something about? Write this down. Now go off and do this.

6) Repeat step 5 until you've totally confronted the problem.

7) Go back to step number 2 and choose the next problem that is now the easiest for you to confront. Do steps 3 through 6.

8) Continue this until you've totally confronted each part of your relationship that was a problem for you.

What is happening when you do these above steps? You are gradually CONFRONTING the different problems of your relationship.

Do *not* underestimate the effectiveness of this procedure. If you sit down and actually **DO** these 8 steps, you will see significant improvement.

Where All the Problems are Coming From

The reason you have ANY problem areas in life stems from some unwillingness on your part to totally confront that area. When you start the process of confronting that area and then gradually increase your willingness and ability to confront that area, the problems in that area will cease to exist.

Any problem in any area of your life will respond to this technology.

It is interesting to note that some of us feel that life without problems would be a dull and bland existence. Some of us feel that problems are part of the fabric of life and to be problem-free is an "airy-fairy*" proposition.

But I submit that we are much better off if we choose our problems. I like to have some say in the problems I deal with. I submit this is better than having apparently unsolvable problems because we are not willing to totally confront them.

I would prefer the problem of how to take my relationship to the next level, as opposed to how to pull it out of the mud. Which problem would you prefer to confront: what graduation gift to purchase for your son, or when to visit him in prison? I know that sounds a bit brutal, but if you use the technology given in this chapter (and in the rest of this book) you will bring yourself to a position where YOU are choosing life's problems as opposed to life slapping you in the face with them.

In other words, you will be much happier and much more effective if you totally confront the components of your life. You will then be left with the ability to choose what problems you'd like to have.

I am not asking you to totally confront all of your problems all at once. The procedure given in this chapter is designed to help you gradually handle a wide variety of life's problems, including those in your relationships.

Applying this procedure will produce excellent changes. But, as is the case with any workable procedure, you have to actually do it to get the benefits. So, do yourself a favor, turn the pages back and follow the steps all the way through.

Chapter Sixteen

HELP WITH THE KIDS

L. Ron Hubbard developed an extensive amount of technology to help with the rearing of children, which will be the subject matter of a separate book. However, the author could not resist providing some technology here, as the better the parents get along with their children, the better they will get along with each other.

The first tool will take a bit of your time each day, but you will soon find that it's time well spent. Mr. Hubbard says:

> *"Consider, for example, a child of five. The child, from his own viewpoint, has been badly badgered* throughout his short span of years and has been pushed around by the adults. You should provide something which will, in effect be educational first of all. Therefore, set aside a time during the day when the child can do anything he desires which doesn't hurt animals or property. If he wants you around during this time, which you can begin to call 'Billy's time,' fine. Spend the hour or two with him and do whatever he asks you to do, within reason of course. After the novelty wears off he will begin to use 'his' time to ask you questions about the world around him, questions which you should answer very carefully and accurately, no matter what the subject might be. It would be very unfair to say, in answer to an innocent question about sex for instance, 'Now let's don't talk about nasty things like that.' Answer him simply and fully, and with an absolute minimum of stammering and blushing on your part.*
>
> *"Sometimes the child will want to spend 'his' time being held on your lap, and the special case might even want a bottle. Don't tell him this is childish, and that he has outgrown such pursuits. Give him the bottle and hold him on your lap until he tires of this.*
>
> *"Perhaps he will want to dramatize (act out) family difficulties, such as a recent argument between his parents. Fine. Go over it with him just as he*

desires. This will often be beneficial for the child and the parent. When the child becomes assured that there are no strings attached to your offer of 'his' time, he will take full advantage of the opportunity to go over many details which have hurt him, and once returned to in this fashion, they will seldom bother him again.

"Then, after a few periods spent in this way, ask if there is anything he wants to know, or anything he wants to talk about. Allow his dignity and enormous self-determinism to assert itself. Coax him to explain things to you, in his own language. When he runs across something which troubles him for a meaning, he will ask you, if you have gained his confidence. Sometimes when the child asks you a question which you are sure he should have known for some time, feed it back to him as another question, asking him what he thinks about it. This is often what the child really wants, and is only using the question as a means of opening discussion on the subject.

My wife and I used this concept of "own time" with our daughter. We told her that her mom and dad would spend an hour with her every night and that she could do whatever she wanted during that hour. We of course told her that it didn't mean anything harmful nor did it mean that we were committed to spending money during this hour.

She was thrilled. The first three nights we went to Toys R Us. The entire hour her mom and I went down aisle after aisle and she showed us all the different toys she wanted for her birthday. She could stop and spend all the time in the world looking at one particular toy or she could go zipping down each aisle. We were there with her the entire time.

Even if "the child" in her parents came out and we wanted to look at some toy for our delight, we did not (at least we did our best not to). We tried our darndest to be totally there for our daughter. Whatever she wanted to do that hour, that's what we did.

After the third straight night at Toys R Us and while driving home, something very interesting occurred! Our daughter started asking us questions about life. I don't remember the exact questions, but she wanted to know why people acted a certain way. We answered her to the best of our ability and off we went into some very educational conversations.

From my viewpoint, I believe something else was happening here. Our daughter had all this "pent up" desire to see these toys. She wanted to go to Toys R Us real bad and when we told her she had an hour every night that was her time, she didn't give it a second thought. She wanted to go to Toys R Us. And she wanted her mom and dad to go with her. Which was totally fine with us.

After this pent up desire got spent, so to speak, she just sat back and asked us about things going on around her.

Kids do not have a lot of say-so about their time and their space. They are usually told where to be and when to be there. When they find out they can have an entire hour and during that hour they can have total freedom of choice on where to be and what to do—the results are very impressive.

Often a child is pushing against the parents in some way because the child's own self-determinism has been denied. If you not only allow the child his self-determinism, but also encourage it, the child learns to respect the self-determinism of others.

What do you do if you have a bunch of kids? How do you give each of them their own time? If you have three children, you might allow each to have one hour on consecutive nights. Sarah gets her hour on Monday, Bob gets his on Tuesday, Larry on Wednesday and then Sarah again on Thursday. Or maybe you do a half an hour each night with each child. Whatever you work out, realize the purpose of the activity is to give each child his or her time and that it is really their time. As Mr. Hubbard said: "Allow his dignity and enormous self-determinism to assert itself."

Ownership

The subject of a child's possessions is a very important one. How the parent views a child's possessions is also very important. To quote Mr. Hubbard:

> *"A childhood is intensely upset by the subject of ownership since the child is given to understand that he owns certain things and is then commanded in every action he takes with those items. A child cannot have possession, free and clear, of anything in the average family. He is given shoes and is told to take care of them and is punished if he does not take care of them although he apparently owns them. He is given toys and is harassed whenever he abuses them. He finally becomes convinced that he owns nothing and yet he is in a state of anxiety about owning things. Therefore he will try to possess many things and will completely overestimate or underestimate the value of what he has."*

When I first read this quote, I was pretty surprised. I realized that many children do go through this anxiety about ownership! My wife and I decided to apply this to our daughter. When we gave her something, it was HERS. We gave her some ideas on how to take care of that item, but it belonged to HER. If she wanted to take good care of it, that was fine with us. If she wanted to destroy it, well, even if it wasn't fine with us, we did not interfere with her ownership. The item belonged to HER.

If she ruined one of her possessions and wanted a replacement, we explained that we weren't able to do that (although in some cases, we might help her replace an item later on). She pretty quickly realized that if SHE took care of HER items, that they would last an awful lot longer.

How about her room? Well, guess what? We did not force our daughter to clean her room! It was HER room. For some time, it was a pretty messy room. But a day came when she decided that she wanted HER room to look nice. And from that day forward, her room was in much, much better shape.

The most important thing that happened here? SHE used her own self-determinism to change the condition of her living space.

This subject of ownership is very important. If you give your children something, let them truly own it. By all means, give them some advice on how to take care of something, but make sure you let the CHILD be the master of that item's fate! When you implement this piece of data, you may see the child ruin a few things, you may find yourself pulling out a few hairs, but hang in there, this data will bring you a happier and more self determined child. And this will improve things for one and all!

Children and Help

For instance: "enforcing a child to help". Each time my wife and I insisted and even forced our daughter to help, her willingness to help was not really present, and this had an effect on her desire to help the next time. But when we let her help, her willingness and desire to help increased!

How many times does a child want to help with some small detail and we don't quite let the child deliver on this desire to help. Let's say a mom has brought her 4 year old son to the grocery store with her and they are now in the check-out aisle. The 4 year old wants very badly to take one or two items out of the cart and place them on the conveyor belt. He really wants to do this and he sees this as a way of helping mommy. Mommy, however, is pressed for time and the line is moving quickly, so she does not let her son help out. She doesn't quite realize that her 4 year old is doing something very important. He is offering his help!

Children frequently offer their help, and every time the parent refuses it (for whatever reasons), the child's desire to help gets blunted. After a while, the child will find "other ways" to help, which may end up as an upset or disturbance. The parent then wonders what has gotten into the child.

Infallible Parents?

If my wife or I had done something wrong that affected our daughter in some way, we did our best to apologize for that and to point out to her what it was that we did wrong. This was not always easy, but we found it extremely beneficial in the long run. We did not present this infallible image to our daughter. We did not try to convince her that if something went wrong, that her parents were not responsible. To the best of our ability, we explained to her what was happening and this helped increase her trust and respect, two very important qualities.

Bringing up children is one of the most important activities on this planet. When you have workable technology to help you with this, and when this technology is correctly applied, the child can grow and be a true member of the family and eventually the society.

Chapter Seventeen

WHAT IS GREATNESS

by L. Ron Hubbard

> *"The hardest task one can have is to continue to love his fellows despite all reasons he should not.*
>
> *"And the true sign of sanity and greatness is to so continue.*
>
> *"For the one who can achieve this, there is abundant hope.*
>
> *"For those who cannot, there is only sorrow, hatred and despair. And these are not the things of which greatness, or sanity or happiness are made.*
>
> *"A primary trap is to succumb to invitations to hate.*
>
> *"... Sometimes for the sake of safety of others it is necessary to act. But it is not necessary also to hate them.*
>
> *"To do one's task without becoming furious at others who seek to prevent one is a mark of greatness—and sanity. And only then can one be happy.*
>
> *"Seeking to achieve any single desirable quality in life is a noble thing. The one most difficult, and most necessary to achieve, is to love one's fellows despite all invitations to do otherwise.*
>
> *"...True greatness merely refuses to change in the face of bad actions against one—and a truly great person loves his fellows because he understands them.*
>
> *"After all, they are all in the same trap. Some are oblivious* of it, some have gone mad because of it, some act like those who have betrayed them. But all, all are in the same trap—the generals, the street sweepers, the presidents, the insane. They act the way they do because they are subject to the same cruel pressures of this universe.*

"Some of us are subject to those pressures and still go on doing our jobs. Others have long since succumbed and rave and torture and strut like the demented* souls they are.

... "Justice, mercy, forgiveness, all are unimportant beside the ability not to change because of provocation* or demands to do so.

"One must act, one must preserve order and decency, but one need not hate or seek vengeance.

"It is true that beings are frail and commit wrongs. Man is basically good but can act badly.

"He only acts badly when his acts done for order and the safety for others are done with hatred. Or when his disciplines are founded only upon safety for himself regardless of all others; or worse, when he acts only out of a taste for cruelty.

"To preserve no order at all is an insane act. One need only look at the possessions and environment of the insane to realize this. The able keep good order.

"When cruelty in the name of discipline dominates a race, that race has been taught to hate. And that race is doomed.

"The real lesson is to learn to love.

... "Never use what is done to one as a basis for hatred. Never desire revenge.

"It requires real strength to love man. And to love him despite all invitations to do otherwise, all provocations and all reasons why one should not.

"Happiness and strength endure only in the absence of hate. To hate alone is the road to disaster. To love is the road to strength. To love in spite of all is the secret of greatness. And may very well be the greatest secret in this universe."

Chapter Eighteen
CONCLUSION

You now have a variety of tools to help you with your relationships. If you and your partner are having fights, you have procedures to help cool things off (Chapter 6).

If there is a person outside of your relationship actively promoting conflict between you and your partner, the technology in Chapter 5 will help resolve that.

With the technology on overts and withholds in Chapter 4, you can dramatically improve things. Using this technology in connection with past relationships (Chapter 10) will help you flourish in your current relationship. It will also help you start a new relationship.

Learning and using the key components of affinity, reality and communication will bring you and your partner closer together (Chapters 7 and 8).

The Emotional Tone Scale and the Chart of Human Evaluation (Chapters 11, 12 and 13) can help you in virtually every part of a relationship. If you are not currently in an intimate relationship, use the Tone Scale to help you choose a new partner. It could make the total difference between success and failure.

The Tone Scale and the Chart of Human Evaluation can help you predict what people will do and how they will perform. Every facet of a relationship, any relationship, can be better understood.

The more you know about an area of life, the easier it is to be responsible for that area of life. The Knowledge, Responsibility and Control triangle (Chapter 14) provides you with a whole new approach to life's situations.

How important is the ability to confront? Chapter 15 gives you tools to increase this ability. When people avoid problem areas of their life, these problem areas do not disappear, they increase in size ... bringing more stress and unhappiness. Applying the procedures in this Chapter will get things going in the right direction!

And what about our children? Could they use some help? When you treat your child with dignity and respect, you will find more times than not this respect returned. Parents who work on increasing the self determinism of their children will have a saner and more smoothly running household. Chapter 16 provides you with a small helping of advice regarding children. Use what you feel comfortable using and maybe squeeze a little more in each week!

How workable is the material in this book? Thousands of people all over the world have used Mr. Hubbard's technology to improve their relationships. But the key word is **USED**.

In the case of fixing and improving your relationship, I suggest that you take one piece of data in this book and fully apply that one piece. Apply it exactly the way it's recommended and observe for yourself its workability. Then take other pieces of data and put them to work.

Your relationships are very, very important. May they always flourish!

Additional Services Available

We have highly trained counselors available who will come TO YOU and deliver professional marriage counseling based on the works of L. Ron Hubbard.

After marriage counseling success stories:

"As a result of this marriage counseling, we learned what had been causing the trouble for all those years. It's now been 8 years since our marriage counselling and there is no doubt about whether we will make it as a couple. I urge anyone who has any trouble with their marriage, whether great or not so great, to get the marriage counseling based on Mr. Hubbard's technology. It will help you tremendously." —G.C.

"The marriage counseling was totally awesome. We were headed for a break-up of our marriage or at the very least a minimal co-existence in the same household which was not only devastating to both of us but also creating chaos in the family with our 2 girls. We went through the counseling and now have restored communication between us as well as love. We haven't had a cross word with each other and we have noticed feeling peaceful. The effects on the rest of the household have also been very positive. This was definitely worth the money and the effort. Our counselor was friendly, professional, compassionate, patient and knowledgeable." —V.L.

The full program takes between 5-7 days.
Call **1-888-917-8223** for more information.

Or contact us in the following ways:
Email: SRDubin@aol.com / Fax: 727-441-9303
By mail: Center for Personal Enhancement
1858 Feathertree Circle • Clearwater, FL 33765

Glossary

acknowledgement: something said or done to inform another that his statement or action has been noted, understood and received. "Very good," "Okay," and other such phrases are intended to inform another who has spoken or acted that his statement or action has been accepted. - L. Ron Hubbard

acute: an acute illness becomes severe very quickly but does not last very long. (compare chronic)

administer: to give or hand out formally; to provide.

affinity: the feeling of love or liking for something or someone. - L. Ron Hubbard

airy-fairy: if you describe someone's ideas as airy-fairy, you are criticizing them because you think they are vague, impractical and unrealistic.

apparency: a situation, quality, or feeling that seems to exist, although you cannot be certain that it does exist.

appeasement: if you try to appease someone, you try to stop them from being angry by giving them what they want; often used showing disapproval.

ascertain: to discover or find out something.

badgered: to be repeatedly told to do something or repeatedly asked questions.

badlands: an area of rocks and hills where no crops can be grown.

being: the personality which actually is the individual and is aware of being aware and is ordinarily and normally the "person" and who the individual thinks he is. - L. Ron Hubbard

breadth: a wide range or variety.

chronically: a chronic illness or disability lasts for a very long time. You can describe someone's bad habits or behaviour as chronic when they have behaved like that for a long time and do not seem to be able to stop themselves. (compare acute)

common denominator: a common denominator is a characteristic or attitude that is shared by all members of a group.

consciousness: the condition of being awake and understanding what is happening around you.

control: when we say control, we simply mean willingness to start, stop and change. - L. Ron Hubbard / To make someone or something do what you want or work in a particular way.

covert: covert activities or situations are secret or hidden.

damp: to deaden the vibration of (a piano string, drum membrane, etc.)

demented: behaving in a way that is crazy or very strange.

derogatory: if you make a derogatory remark or comment, you express your low opinion of someone or something.

discreditable: discreditable behaviour is not acceptable because people consider it to be shameful and wrong.

disintegration: if something disintegrates, it becomes seriously weakened, and is divided or destroyed.

dolefully: a doleful expression, manner or voice is depressing and miserable.

elicit: to get information, a reaction, etc. from someone.

embroiled: if someone embroils you in a fight or an argument, they get you deeply involved in it.

enturbulate: cause to be agitated and disturbed. - L. Ron Hubbard

enunciate: when you enunciate a thought, idea, or plan, you express it very clearly and precisely.

equilateral: (regarding a triangle) having all sides equal.

ethics: ethics has to do with a code of agreement amongst people that they will conduct themselves in a fashion which will attain to the optimum solution of their problems. - L. Ron Hubbard

evaluate: telling the person what to think. - L. Ron Hubbard

evaluation (as in Chart of Human Evaluation) if you evaluate something or someone, you consider them in order to make a judgement about them, for example about how good or bad they are.

extroversion: extroversion means nothing more than being able to look outward. The person ceasing to put attention on his mind, but putting his attention on the environment. - L. Ron Hubbard

fixedly: if you stare fixedly at something, you look at it steadily and continuously for a period of time.

grips: come to grips: if you come to grips with a problem, you consider it seriously, and start taking action to deal with it.

hypothesize: if you hypothesize that something will happen, you say that you think that thing will happen because of various facts you have considered.

impending: likely to happen soon.

inaccessible: if something is inaccessbile, you are unable to see, use or buy it.

inclination: an inclination is a feeling that makes you want to act in a particular way.

infallible: if a person or thing is infallible, they are never wrong.

infomercial: an infomercial is a television program in which a famous person gives information about a company's products or services. The word is formed from 'information' and 'commercial'.

interrelationship: a close relationship between two or more things or people.

invalidate: to refute or discredit or deny something that someone else considers a fact. - L. Ron Hubbard

ivory tower: if you describe someone as living in an ivory tower, you disapprove of them because you think they have no knowledge or experience of the practical problems of everyday life.

knack: habit of doing something.

knowledge: that which is known, information, instruction; enlightenment, learning; practical skill. Whatever can be thought about or perceived. - L. Ron Hubbard

knuckle under: if you knuckle under, you do what someone else tells you to do or what a situation forces you to do.

matching: if something such as an amount or quality matches with another, or if the two things match, they are both the same or equal.

mechanics: the mechanics of a process, system or activity are the way in which it works or the way in which it is done.

mechanism: a way in which something works or the process by which it is done.

medium: a medium is a way or means of expressing your ideas or communicating with people.

nook and cranny: if you talk about every nook and cranny of a place or situation, you mean every part or every aspect of it.

notch: you can refer to a step on a scale of measurement or achievement as a notch.

oblivious: if you are oblivious to something, you are not aware of it.

omission: an omission is something that has not been included or has not been done. It is also the act of not including someone or something or of not doing something.

party: one of the people or groups involved in an argument, agreement, etc.

perpetrator: the person who commits a crime or any other immoral or harmful act.

physiology: the physiology of a human or animal's body is the way that it functions.

precipitate: if something precipitates an event or situation, usually a bad one, it causes it to happen suddenly or sooner than normal.

prolific: a prolific writer, artist or composer produces a large number of works.

propitiation: the strange manifestation of the individual attempting to buy off imagined danger. People who are far down the Tone Scale will, when they reach 1.0 (fear), quite commonly offer someone presents and attempt to do things for them.

provocation: an action or event that makes someone angry, or that is intended to do this.

psychobabble: you can use psychobabble to refer to complicated language, especially language relating to psychoanalysis, which is used in a meaningless way.

punitive: punitive actions are intended to punish people.

rationale: the rationale for a course of action, practice or belief is the set of reasons on which it is based.

realization: if you realize that something is true, you become ware that fact or understand it.

rehabilitate: to rehabilitate something means to improve its condition.

reiterate: to say something more than once.

responsibility: willingness to own or act; being able to care for, ro reach; to admit causing. - L. Ron Hubbard

restrain: if you restrain an emotion or impulse, you prevent yourself from showing that emotion or doing what you intended to do.

scathing: scathing remarks, comments, etc. criticize someone or something very severely.

scenario: if you talk about a likely or possible scenario, you are talking about the way in which a situation may develop.

solvent: something that solves. To **solve**: to find the solution to; provide an answer for.

spot: if you spot someone or something, you notice them.

strained: unfriendly, uncomfortable, and showing a lack of trust.

subversives: people who attempt to weaken or destroy a political system or government.

succomb: if you succomb to persuasion or to a desire for something, you are unable to resist it although you feel it may be wrong.

sulks: if you sulk, you are silent and bad-tempered because you are annoyed about something.

supplication: a prayer or request to God or someone in authority for help.

sympathetic vibration: a vibration caused by other vibrations transmitted from a neighboring body.

sympathy: the posing of any emotion so as to be similar to the emotion of another. - L. Ron Hubbard

tit-for-tat: a tit-for-tat crime or action is something bad that has been done to someone because he/she has done something similar to you.

tone scale: (see Chapter 13) a scale which shows the successive emotional tones a person can experience. By 'tone' is meant the momentary or continuing emotional states of a person. - L. Ron Hubbard

trauma: trauma is a very severe shock or very upsetting experience.

tuning fork: a small steel instrument with two prongs, which when struck sounds a certain fixed tone. It is most commonly used in tuning musical instruments.

validate: to validate a person is to confirm that he/she is valuable or worthwhile.

vertebrae: the small circular bones that form the backbone of a human being or animal.

victimized: if someone is victimized, they are deliberately treated unfairly.

Victorian: Victorian means belonging to, connected with, or typical of Britain in the middle and last parts of the 19th century, when Victoria was queen. You can use Victorian to describe pepole who have old-fashioned qualities, especially in relation to discipline and morals.

vitality: life and energy.

word processor: a computer or computer program which is used to produce printed material such as documents, letters, and books.

Order Form

Email: SRDubin@aol.com
Fax Orders:
1-727-441-9303
(Fax this order form)

Telephone Orders:
Call Toll Free
1-888-917-8223
(Have your credit card ready)

Mail Orders:
Workable Solutions
1858 Feathertree Circle
Clearwater, FL 33765
(Mail form with order)

PLEASE SEND THE FOLLOWING BOOKS:

Technology of Study Booklet   Cost: $ 5.00   Copies: _____   Amt: _____

Answers to Drugs Booklet   Cost: $ 5.00   Copies: _____   Amt: _____

The Way to Happiness Booklet   Cost: $ 3.00   Copies: _____   Amt: _____

Science of Survival   Cost: $50.00   Copies: _____   Amt: _____
by L. Ron Hubbard
Detailed presentation of the Hubbard Chart of Human Evaluation.
Learn how to predict the behavior of *all* those you come into contact with.

The Small Business Success Manual   Cost: $28.95   Copies: _____   Amt: _____
Full set of tools based on L. Ron Hubbard's works. Learn how to increase
business income *while* reducing stress.

The Special Course in Human Evaluation Cost: $325.00   Copies _____   Amt: _____
Series of lectures given by L. Ron Hubbard. Learn how to effectively use
the tone scale in every phase of your life. (Audio Cassettes)

When TheThrill Is Gone (add'l copies)   Cost: $28.95   Copies: _____   Amt: _____

Subtotal: _____

Add 6% for materials shipped to Florida addresses: **Sales tax:** _____

Shipping (U.S. rates):

$2.00 for each <u>booklet</u> shipped.   _____

$4.50 to ship each copy of The Small Business Success Manual.   _____

$4.50 to ship each copy of When The Thrill Is Gone.   _____

$5.50 to ship each copy of Science of Survival.   _____

$8.50 to ship The Special Course in Human Evaluation.   _____

Total: _____

Name _____   Telephone _____

Address _____

City _____   State _____   Zip _____

Payment Options:

☐ Check   ☐ Money Order   ☐ VISA   ☐ MasterCard   ☐ AMEX   ☐ Discover

Card Number: _____

Name on Card: _____   Expiration Date _____

Signature (for credit card orders): _____